HISTORY OF ART
ANCIENT ART

HISTORY OF ART
Volume I   ANCIENT ART
Volume II   MEDIÆVAL ART   (*In Preparation*)
Volume III   RENAISSANCE ART "   "
Volume IV   MODERN ART   "   "

ELIE FAURE
HISTORY OF ART

ANCIENT ART

Translated from the French by
WALTER PACH

*Illustrated from Photographs
Selected by the Author*

HARPER & BROTHERS PUBLISHERS
NEW YORK AND LONDON

History of Art—Ancient Art

Copyright, 1921, by Harper & Brothers
Printed in the United States of America

I–λ̄

To My Wife

Pompeian mosaic (*Museum of Naples*).

TABLE OF CONTENTS

CHAPTER		PAGE
	Translator's Preface	ix
	Introduction to the First French Edition (1909)	xvii
	Preface to the New Edition (1920)	xxxv
I.	Before History	3
II.	Egypt	31
III.	The Ancient Orient	78
IV.	The Sources of Greek Art	113
V.	Phidias	149
VI.	The Dusk of Mankind	187
VII.	Intimate Greece	229
VIII.	Rome	263
	Alphabetical Index	305
	Synoptic Tables	307
	Signs and Abbreviations	309

TRANSLATOR'S PREFACE

ART history is, in its essentials, the history of man, for no one can write the story of art in more than a superficial way without following out the relation of each school to the ideas of its period and its people. But it is even more than that: it is the history of the development of man as revealed by his art. Elie Faure, in the present history, pursues this idea with a fidelity and an understanding that it has never received till now. Indeed, one may almost say that such a work as this could not have been written earlier, for it has been only gradually that we have come to understand the relation of art to the character and surroundings of the races it represents. Various works on isolated artists and schools have dealt with their subject from this standpoint, but there existed no survey of the world's art as a whole until the four volumes of this series were written.

The professional, whether critic, teacher, or artist, will find in these pages the fullest application of the modern theory of history (for the governing idea here is one that goes beyond the limits of art history), while the layman will follow the epic of man's development in company with a passionate lover of beauty who has the gift of communicating his enthusiasm. It is a fallacy to believe that a book for the general reader should dilute the ideas of works addressed to specialists. The contrary is true: to meet the needs of persons of diverse interests, more intensity of idea is required, more breadth of scope, than is demanded of a treatise for specialists, whose concern with their subject will cause them to overlook dryness and diffuseness if a valuable theory is established or new facts are arrived at.

For a comparison of the older and the newer views of art history, the reader can scarcely be referred to anything clearer than M. Faure's own discussion in the preface to the new edition of this work (page xxxv). His brief reference there to the synoptic tables at the back of each volume may be supplemented by the assurances received from various close students of the special schools and epochs, who agree in vouching for the thoroughness with which this most objective compilation of names and dates has been made. A reference chart is thus constantly before the reader, serving him as a road map does a traveler. The text of most art histories does little more than amplify such tables. The characteristic which distinguishes Elie Faure's *History of Art* is that it shows the mass of facts functionally—as the living brain and heart of mankind.

The loyalty with which, in the preface mentioned, M. Faure defends the work of the archæologist is due in part to his appreciation of the material that the searchers for detail have placed at his disposal, but doubtless in part also to the fact that he himself knows the labor of obtaining the first-hand information on which the history and interpretation of art are built. At no one place, however (and one need not fear to lay too much stress on this point), does he fall into the error of imagining that an assembling of facts is history. Even when writing of arts like the Egyptian and the Greek, as to which his study on the historic sites has given him a special authority, even when treating of the Gothic period, as to which his knowledge is so profound as to make Mr. Havelock Ellis apply the word "unsurpassable" to the chapters of this history on Gothic art—his modern understanding of his task causes him to refer constantly to the philosophy, social life, and ideals of the people under examination, and not to their art alone. He goes farther, and by a series of dramatic confrontations makes us realize the differences among the arts and their debt to one another. Thus, in the pages on the Gothic he has before his eyes the color of Mohammedan art which was of such importance to western Europe when its returning crusaders brought back to the glassmakers of the cathedrals their memories of the Orient. Yet M. Faure's main guide in this part of his study is the life of the mediæval commune; he shows its relation to the appearance or nonappearance of great cathedrals in the French cities and its use as a basis for an explanation of the difference between English and French Gothic. We are thus relieved in very large measure from the tyranny of taste and of arbitrary assertion that plays so large a part in most art writing.

In the present volume, again, the rise and decline of Greek art are not treated as matters that have been permanently decided by experts; neither does the author justify his statements in terms of æsthetics to be followed only by those persons who have had a special experience in the arts. The sources of Greek art are studied with a view of allowing anyone interested in the subject to see the reason for the "focus" that would be produced when the elements of the light were fused, the golden period is considered with relation to the ideas of philosophy and liberty which had so great an effect on the arts, and as Greece turns to the Dusk of Mankind (with which variant of Wagner's word "Götterdämmerung" M. Faure entitles his chapter on the decline), we are again shown, in the ideas at work in the race, the reasons for the new phases of its art—and not simply told that one statue is later or worse than another, or involved in technical intricacies from which we only escape with the classic "*de gustibus.*"

A feature of the history, which, the English reader will recognize with the four volumes before him, is the scope of the work. It is one of the proofs of its right to represent the modern idea of art. Beginning with the accessions to our knowledge a century ago, when important Greek works came to northern Europe, we have for a hundred years been extending the boundaries of the art considered classic. The masterpieces of Japan, China, and India have been reaching us only since the middle of the nineteenth century. The last of the exotic arts to affect Europeans has been that of the African sculptors. No other history approaches that of M. Faure in its full and clear

TRANSLATOR'S PREFACE

study of the contribution of these more lately recognized arts to the widening of our horizon and to the changes in our understanding which they have caused.

It is not alone that the art of the last half century is different from that of earlier times because it is built on a wider base, but that to-day we see the whole of the past with new eyes. As our thought evolves there will unquestionably be further changes in our estimate of the past, but the summary resulting from the present work may confidently be expected to hold its rank as an important one in the history of the subject. For we have here the ideas of a period of intense research and criticism, and a point in that period when our thought has attained at least a temporary tranquillity through its grasp of the new elements at its command and through an outlook on art that represents the creative men of the epoch.

It is to be doubted whether later critics will differ, to a radical degree, from the judgment of the Renaissance to which M. Faure points in his volume on that period, for the great critical activity of the last half century has been specially occupied with the Renaissance, and M. Faure knows well the results of this study. Perhaps it will be around the volume on *Modern Art* that later discussion will mainly center, for here the currents of interpretation sometimes issue from conflicting sources. M. Faure's analysis, however, must have a permanent interest, for it is based on too deep an understanding of the political and social structure of the European countries ever to be entirely superseded. It is the philosophy of a man whose role in the drama of his time is enriched by the great breadth of his activities and who has drawn on them all in his writing on art—the central interest of his career.

Elie Faure is a physician, and the scientist's knowledge and point of view is to be traced in his *History of Art* as well as in his masterly essay on Lamarck. He is one of the founders of the Université Populaire and one of its lecturers. The thought on social questions which informs those books by M. Faure that treat of economic and racial evolution, of ethics and of war, recurs when he writes of art, or rather he looks on all of these things as inextricably mingled.

As we reach his pages on the later nineteenth century and the twentieth (for the last volume carries us to the art produced since the war), we find the author giving not only the original judgments that characterize his history from its beginning, but transmitting to us the ideas of the artists themselves, for as a result of his personal acquaintance with many of the chief workers of his time, he is enabled to speak not only of them but for them.

And yet the tone of these pages is but little different from that of the remainder of the work; the arts of the past have been so alive for the writer that his words seem to come most often from one who had seen the work produced. While searching untiringly for the facts of history and presenting their essentials in the order and relationship that the most modern scholarship has made available, the idea behind the

TRANSLATOR'S PREFACE

whole work must (as M. Faure himself explains in the preface to the new edition before cited) be tinged with the personality of the writer and by the character of his time. "The historian who calls himself a scientist simply utters a piece of folly." In these matters judgment is inevitable, for to write the history of art one must make one's decisions as to what it is. The writing of it is in itself a work of art—as the style of Elie Faure is there to prove. Only one who feels the emotions of art can tell others which are the great works and make clear the collective poem formed by their history. It is precisely because Elie Faure is adding something to that poem that he has the right to tell us of its meaning.

WALTER PACH.

INTRODUCTION TO THE FIRST FRENCH EDITION (1909)

ART, which expresses life, is as mysterious as life. It escapes all formulas, as life does. But the need of defining it pursues us, because it enters every hour of our existence, aggrandizing the aspects of that existence by its more elevated forms or dishonoring them by its lower forms. No matter how distasteful it is for us to make the effort to hear and to observe, it is impossible for us not to hear and to see, it is impossible for us to refrain wholly from forming some kind of opinion of the world of appearances —the meaning of which it is precisely the mission of art to reveal to us. Historians, moralists, biologists, and metaphysicians—all those who demand of life the secret of its origins and its purposes—are sooner or later compelled to ask why we recognize ourselves in the works which manifest life. But the too restricted limits of biology, of metaphysics, of morality, and of history compel us to narrow the field of our vision when we enter the moving immensity of the poem that man sings, forgets, and has begun again to sing and to forget ever since he has been man. It matters not which of these studies has interested us, the feeling for beauty will be found to be identical in all of them. And without doubt it is this feeling that dominates them and draws them on to that possible unity which is the goal of human activity and which alone makes that activity real.

It is only by listening to the heart that one can speak of art without belittling it. We are all, in some measure, partakers of the truth, but we cannot know truth itself, unless we desire passionately to seek it out and, having found it, feel the enthusiasm to proclaim it widely. Only he who permits the divine voices to sing within him knows how to respect the mystery of the work which inspired him to induce other men to share in his emotion. Michelet did not betray the Gothic workmen or Michael Angelo, because he himself was consumed by the passion which uplifts the nave of the cathedrals and that other passion which unchains its storm in the vaults of the Sistine. Baudelaire was a great poet because he penetrated to the central hearth from which the spirit of the heroes radiates in force and in light. Moreover, if the ideas of Taine did not die with him, it is because his artist's nature is greater than his will and because his dogmatic stiffness is continually over-

INTRODUCTION xix

flowed by the incessantly renewed wave of sensations and of images.

Taine came at the hour when we learned that our own destiny was bound up with the acts of those who have preceded us on life's road and even with the very structure of the earth from which we spring. He was, therefore, in a position to see the form of our thought issue from the mold of history. "Art sums up life." It enters us with the strength of our soil, the color of our sky, through the atavistic preparation which determines it, as well as through the passions and the will of men—which it defines. For the expression of our ideas, we employ the materials which our eyes can see and our hands touch. It is impossible that Phidias, the sculptor who lived in the South, in a clearly defined world, and Rembrandt, the painter who lived in the mist of the North, amid a floating world—two men separated by twenty centuries during which humanity lived, suffered, and aged—should use the same words. Only, it is necessary that we should recognize ourselves in Rembrandt as well as in Phidias.

Not until we have expressed in some sort of language the appearance of the things about us do these things exist for us and retain their appearance. If art were nothing more than a reflection of societies, which pass like shadows of clouds upon the earth, we should ask no more of art than that it teach us history. But it recounts man to us, and, through him, the universe. It goes beyond the moment, it lengthens the duration of time, it widens the comprehension of man, and extends the life and limit of the universe. It fixes moving eternity in its momentary form.

In recounting man to us, art teaches us to know and understand ourselves. The strange thing is that there should be any need for art to do this. Tolstoi's book [1] meant nothing else. He came at a painful moment when, strongly fortified by the results of our research work, but bewildered by the horizons which it opened, we perceived that our effort was becoming diffused, and sought to compare the results attained in order to unite in a common faith and march forward. We think and believe what we need to think and to believe, and it is this which gives to our thoughts and beliefs, throughout our history, that indestructible foundation of humanity which they all have. Tolstoi said what it was necessary to say at the moment when he said it.

Art is the appeal to the instinct of communion in men. We recognize one another by the echoes it awakens in us, which we transmit to others by our enthusiasm, and which resound in the deeds of men throughout all generations, even when those generations may not suspect it. If, during the hours of depression and lack of comprehension only a few of us hear the call, it is that in those hours we alone possess the idealistic energy which later is to reanimate the heroism asleep in the multitudes. It has been said that the artist is sufficient unto himself. That is not true. The artist who says so is infected with an evil pride. The artist who believes it is not an

[1] Tolstoi, *What is Art?*

artist. If he had not needed the most universal of our languages, the artist would not have created it. He would dig the ground to get his bread on a desert island. No one has more need of the presence and approbation of men. He speaks because he feels their presence around him, and lives in the hope—sometimes despaired of but never relinquished—that they will come at last to understand him. It is his function to pour out his being, to give as much as he can of his life, to demand of others that they also give him as much as they can of themselves, to realize with them—in an obscure and magnificent collaboration—a harmony all the more impressive that a greater number of lives have participated in it. The artist, to whom men give everything, returns in full measure what he has taken from them.

Nothing touches us except what happens to us or what can happen to us. The artist is ourselves. He has behind him the same depths of humanity, whether enthusiastic or depressed; he has about him the same secret nature, which each of his steps broadens. The artist is the crowd, to which we all belong, which defines us all, with our consent or despite our resistance. He has not the power to gather up the stones of the house which he builds us (at the risk of crushing in his breast and of tearing his hands), on any road save that on which we travel at his side. He must suffer from that which makes our suffering, and we must make him suffer. He must feel our joys and he must derive them from us. It is necessary that he live our griefs and our inner victories, even when we do not feel them.

The artist can feel and dominate his surroundings only when he considers them as a means of creation. Only then does he give us those permanent realities which all acts and all moments reveal to those who know how to see and how to live. These realities survive the changes in human society as the mass of the sea survives the agitations of its surface. Art is always a "system of relations," and a synthetic system. This is true even of primitive art, which shows the passionate pursuit of an essential sentiment, despite its indefatigable accumulation of detail. Every image symbolizes in brief the idea which the artist creates for himself of the unlimited world of sensations and forms. Every image is an expression of his desire to bring about in this world the reign of that order which he knows how to discover in it. Art has been, since its most humble origins, the realization of the presentiments of certain men—who answer the needs of all men. Art has forced the world to yield to it the laws which have permitted us to establish progressively the sovereignty of our mind over the world. Emanating from humanity, art has revealed to humanity its own intelligence. Art has defined the races; alone it bears the testimony of their dramatic effort. If we want to know what we are, we must understand what art is.

Art initiates us into certain profound realities whose actual possession would enable humanity to bring about, within and around, itself the supreme harmony which is the fugitive goal of its endeavor; we do not desire such possession, however, as its effect would

INTRODUCTION

be to kill movement and thereby kill hope. Art is surely something infinitely greater than it is imagined to be by those who do not understand it. Perhaps also it is more practical than is thought by many of those who feel the force of its action. Born of the association of our sensibility and our experience, formed in order that we may be the masters of ourselves, it has, at all events, nothing of that disinterested aloofness to which Kant, Spencer, and Guyau himself attempted to limit its sphere. All the images in the world are useful instruments for us, and the work of art attracts us only because we recognize in it the formulation of our desire.

We admit freely that objects of primary utility—our clothing, our furniture, our vehicles, our roads, our houses—seem to us beautiful when they serve their purpose adequately. But we stoutly persist in placing above—that is, outside of Nature, the superior organisms in which she proclaims herself—our bodies, our faces, our thoughts, the infinite world of ideas, of passions, and of the landscapes in which these organisms live, and by which they are mutually defined—so that we are unable to separate them. Guyau did not go far enough when he asked himself if the most useful gesture were not the most beautiful, and with him we recoil from the decisive word as if it would stifle our dream. Yet we know our dream to be imperishable, since we shall never attain that realization of ourselves which we pursue unceasingly. Let me quote a sentence uttered by him among all men whose intelligence was freest, perhaps, from any material limitation: "Is it not the function of a beautiful body," said Plato, "is it not its utility which demonstrates to us that it is beautiful? And everything which we find beautiful—faces, colors, sounds, professions—are not all these beautiful in the measure that we find them useful?"

Let our idealism be reassured! It is only by a long accumulation of emotion and of will that man reaches the point on life's road where he can recognize the forms which are useful to him. It is this choice alone, made by certain minds, which will determine for the future, in the instincts of multitudes, what is destined to pass from the domain of speculation into the domain of practice. It is our general development, it is the painful but constant purification of our intelligence and of our desire, which create and render necessary certain forms of civilization—which positive minds translate into the direct and easy satisfaction of all their material needs. What is most useful to man is the idea.

The beautiful form, whether it be a tree or a river, the breasts of a woman or her sides, the shoulders or arms of a man, or the cranium of a god—the beautiful form is the form that adapts itself to its function. The idea has no other role than that of defining the form for us. The idea is the lofty outlook and the infinite extension in the world and in the future of the most imperious of our instincts. It sums up and proclaims this instinct as the flower and the fruit sum up the plant, prolong it and perpetuate it. Every being, even the lowest, contains within himself, at least once in his earthly adventure—when he loves—all the poetry of the world. And he whom we call the artist is the one among living beings who, in the presence of universal life, maintains the state of love in his heart.

The obscure and formidable voice which reveals to man and to woman the beauty of woman and man, and impels them to make a decisive choice so that they may perpetuate and perfect their species, never ceases to resound in the artist, strengthened and multiplied by all the voices and the murmurs and the sounds and the tremblings which accompany it. That voice—he is forever hearing it, every time that the grasses move, every time that a violent or graceful form proclaims its life along his pathway. He hears it as he follows, from the roots to the leaves, the rise of the sap from under the earth to the trunks and the branches of the trees, every time that he looks at the sea rising and falling as if to respond to the tide of billions of life-cells that roll in it, every time that the fructifying force of heat and rain overwhelms him, every time that the generating winds repeat to him that human hymns are made up of the calls to voluptuousness and hope with which the world is filled. He seeks out the forms which he foresees, as a man or an animal in the grip of love seeks them. His desire passes from one form to another, he compares them pitilessly, and from his comparisons there springs forth, one day, the superior form, the idea whose recollection will weigh on his heart so long as he has not imparted his own life to it. He suffers until death, because each time that he has made a form fruitful, brought an idea to light, the image of another is born in him, and because his hope, never wearied of reaching out for what he desires, can only be born of the despair at not having attained his desire. He suffers; his tyrannical disquietude often makes those around him suffer. But around him, and fifty centuries after him, he consoles millions of men. The work he will leave behind him will assure an increase of power to those who can understand the logic and the certitude of his images. In listening to him, men will enjoy the illusion which he enjoyed for a moment—the illusion, often formidable but always ennobling, of absolute adaptation.

It is the only divine illusion! We give the name of a god to the form which best interprets our desire—sensual, moral, individual, social, no matter what,—our vague desire to comprehend, to utilize life, ceaselessly to extend the limits of the intelligence and the heart. With this desire we invade the lines, the projections, and the volumes which proclaim this form to us, and it is in the meeting with the powerful forces that circulate within the form that the god reveals himself to us. From the impact of the spirit that animates the form with the spirit that animates us, life springs forth. We shall never be able to utilize it unless it responds wholly to those obscure movements which dictate our own actions. Rodin sees quivering in the block of marble a man and a woman knotted together by their arms and their legs, but we shall never understand the tragic necessity for such an embrace if we do not feel that an inner force, desire, mingles the hearts and the flesh of the bodies thus welded together. When Carrière wrests from the matter of the universe a mother giving the breast to her child, we shall not understand the value of that union if we do not feel that an inner force, love, dictates the bending of the torso and the curve of the mother's arm, and that another inner force, hunger, buries the infant in her bosom. The image that expresses nothing is not beautiful, and the finest sentiment escapes us if it does not directly determine the image which shall translate it. The pediments, frescoes, and epics, the symphonies, the loftiest architectures, all the sweep of liberty, the glory and the irresistible power of the infinite and living temple which we erect to ourselves, are in this mysterious accord.

In every case, it is this agreement which defines all the higher forms of the testimonies to confidence and faith which we have left on our long road. It defines all our idealistic effort, which no finalism—in the "radical"[1] sense which the philosophers are giving to the world—has directed. Our idealism is no other thing than the reality of our mind. The necessity of adaptation creates it and maintains it in us, that it may be increased and transmitted to our children. It exists as a possibility at the foundation of our original moral life, as the physical man is contained in the distant protozoan. Our research for the absolute is the indefatigable desire for the repose that

---

[1] H. Bergson, *Creative Evolution*.

would result from our decisive triumph over the group of blind forces which oppose our progress. But, for our salvation, the farther we go, the more distant the goal becomes. The goal of life is living, and it is to ever-moving and ever-renewing life that our ideal leads us.

When we follow the march of time and pass from one people to another, the forms of that ideal seem to change. But what changes, basically, is the needs of a given time or the needs of given peoples whose future alone can show, across the variations of appearances, the identity of their nature and the character of their usefulness to us. Scarcely have we left the Egypto-Hellenic world before we see, stretching before us like a plain, the kingdom of the mind. The temples of the Hindoos and the cathedrals break into its frontiers, the cripples of Spain and the poor of Holland invade it without introducing even one of those types of general humanity through which the first artists had defined our needs. What does it matter? The great dream of humanity can recognize, there again, the effort toward adaptation which has always guided it. Other conditions of life have appeared, different forms of art have made us feel the necessity for understanding them in order to direct us in the path of our best interests. Real landscape, the life of the people, and the life of the middle class, arrive and powerfully characterize the aspects of every day, into which our soul, exhausted with its dream, may retire and refresh itself. The appeal of misery and despair, even, is made, that we may get back to ourselves, know ourselves, and strengthen ourselves.

If we turn to the Egyptians, to the Assyrians, the Greeks, the Hindoos, the French of the Middle Ages, the Italians, and the Dutch, one after the other, it is that we belong now to one group of surroundings, now to one epoch, now to one minute, even of our time or of our life, which has need of a given people more than of another one. When we are cold we seek the sun; we seek the shadow when we are warm. The great civilizations which have formed us are each entitled to an equal share of our gratitude, because we have successively asked of each the things we lacked. We have lived tradition when it was to our interest to live it, and have accepted revolution when it saved us. We have been idealists when the world was abandoning itself to discouragement or was foreseeing new destinies, realists when it seemed to have found its provisional stability. We have not asked for more reserve from passionate races or more ardor from positive races, because we have understood the necessity of passion and the necessity of the positive spirit. It is we who wrote the immense book wherein Cervantes has recounted our generous enthusiasm and our practical common sense. We have followed one or the other of the great currents of the mind, and we have been able to invoke arguments of almost equal value to justify our inclinations. What we call idealistic art, what we call realistic art, are momentary forms of our eternal action. It is for us to seize the immortal moment when the forces of conservation and the forces of revolution in life marry, for the realization of the equilibrium of the human soul.

Thus, whatever the form in which a thing is offered to us, whether true now or true in our desire, or true both in its immediate appearance and in its possible destinies, the object by itself and the fact by itself are nothing. They count only through their infinitely numerous relationships with infinitely complex surroundings. And it is these relationships, never twice the same, which translate universal feelings of an infinite simplicity. Each fragment of the work, because it is adapted to its end, however humble that end may be, must extend itself in silent echoes throughout the whole of the depth and breadth of the work. Its sentimental tendencies are, in reality, secondary: "Beautiful painting," said Michael Angelo, "is religious in itself, for the soul is elevated by the effort it has to make to attain perfection and to mingle with God; beautiful painting is a reflection of that divine perfection, a shadow from the brush of God . . . !"

Idealistic or realistic, a thing of the present day or of general conditions, let the work live, and in order to live, let it be *one*, first of all! The work which has not this oneness dies, like the ill-formed creatures which the species, evolving toward higher destinies, must eliminate little by little. The work which is one, on the contrary, lives in the least of its fragments. The breast of an ancient statue, a foot, an arm, even when half devoured by subterranean moisture, quivers and seems warm to the touch of the hand, as if vital forces were still modeling it from within. The unearthed fragment is alive. It bleeds like a wound. Over the gulf of the centuries, the mind finds its relations with the pulverized debris, it animates the organism as a whole with an existence which is imaginary, but present to our emotion. It is the magnificent testimony to the human importance of art, engraving the effort of our intelligence on the seats of the earth, as the bones we find there trace the rise of our material organs.

To realize unity in the mind and to transmit it to the work is to obey that need of general and durable order which our universe imposes on us. The scientist expresses this order by the law of continuity, the artist by the law of harmony, the just man by the law of solidarity. These three essential instruments of our human adaptation—science, which defines the relations of fact with fact; art, which suggests the relations of the fact with man; and morality which seeks the relations of man with man—establish for our use, from one end of the material and spiritual world to the other, a system of relations whose permanence and utility demonstrate its logic to us. They teach us what serves us, what harms us. Nothing else matters very greatly. There is neither error nor truth, neither ugliness nor beauty, neither evil nor good outside of the use in human problems which we give to our three instruments. The mission of our sensibility, of our personal intelligence, is to establish the value of them, through searching out, from one to the other, the mysterious passages which will permit us to grasp the continuity of our effort, in order to comprehend and accept it as a whole. By so doing we shall, little by little, utilize what we call error, ugliness, and evil, as means to a higher education and realize harmony in ourselves, that we may extend it about us.

Harmony is a profound law, which goes back to primitive unity, and the desire for it is imposed on us by the most general and the most imperious of all the realities. The forms we see live only through the transitions which unite them. And by these transitions the human mind can return to the common source of the forms, just as it can follow the nourishing current of the sap starting from the flowers and the leaves to go back to the roots. Consider a landscape stretching back to the circle of the horizon. A plain covered with grasses, with clump of trees, a river flowing to the sea, roads bordered with houses, villages, wandering beasts, men, a sky full of light or of clouds. The men feed on the fruit of the trees and on the meat and milk of the beasts, which yield their fur and their skins for clothing. The beasts live on grasses and leaves, and if the grasses and the leaves grow it is because the sky takes from the sea and the rivers the water which it spreads upon them. Neither birth nor death—life, permanent and confused. All aspects of matter interpenetrate one another, general energy is in flux and reflux, it flowers at every moment, to wither and to reflower in endless metamorphoses; the symphony of the colors and the symphony of the murmurs are but little else than the perfume of the inner symphony which issues from the circulation of forces in the continuity of forms.

The artist comes, seizes the universal law, and renders us a world complete, whose elements, characterized by their principal relations, all participate in the harmonious accomplishment of the ensemble of its functions.

Spencer saw the bare heavenly bodies escaping from the nebulæ, solidifying, little by little, the water condensing on their surface, elementary life arising from the water, diversifying its appearances, every day lifting higher its branches, its twigs, its fruits, and, as a spherical flower opens to give its dust to space, the heart of the world expanding in its multiplied forms. But it seems that an obscure desire to return to its origins governs the universe. The planets, issue of the sun, cannot tear themselves from its encircling force, though they seem to want to plunge back into it. Atom solicits atom, and all living organisms, coming from the same cell, seek living organisms to make that cell again through burying themselves in each other. . . . Thus the just man contents himself with living, thus the scientist and the artist delve into the world of forms and feelings and cause their consciousness to retrace its steps along the road which that world traveled, to pass from its ancient homogeneity to its present diversity. And thus, in a heroic effort, they re-recreate primitive unity.

Let the artist, therefore, be proud of his life of illumination and of pain. Of these heralds of hope he plays the greatest role. In every case he can attain this role. Scientific activity, social activity bear within themselves a signification sufficiently defined for them to be self-sufficient. Art touches science through the world of forms, which is the element of its work, it enters the social plane by addressing itself to our faculty of love. There are great savants who cannot arouse emotion in us, men of great honesty who cannot reason. There is no hero of art who is not at the same time (through the sharp and long conquest of his means of expression) a hero of knowledge and a human hero of the heart. When he feels living within him the earth and space and all that moves and all that lives, even all that seems dead—to the very tissue of the stones—how could it be that he should not feel the life of the emotions, the passions, the sufferings of those who are made as he is? Whether he knows it or not, whether he wants it or not, his art is of a piece with the work of the artists of yesterday and the artists of to-morrow; it reveals to the men of to-day the solidarity of their effort. All action in time, all action in space have their goal in his action. It is his place to affirm the agreement of the thought of Jesus, of the thought of Newton, and of the thought of Lamarck. And it is on that account that Phidias and Rembrandt must recognize each other and that we must recognize ourselves in them.

PREFACE TO THE NEW EDITION (1920)

I HAVE been on the point of suppressing the pages which serve as an *Introduction* to the first edition of this book. I judged them—I still judge them—boyish and tearful in their philosophy, and obscure and badly written as well. I have given up my intention. After all, those pages represent a moment of myself. And since I have attempted to express that moment, it no longer belongs to me.

Perhaps one ought to write works composed of several volumes in a few months, their documentation once finished and the ideas they represent having been thoroughly set in order. The unity of the work would gain thereby. But the ensemble of the worker's effort would doubtless lose. Every time he thinks he has been mistaken, a living desire awakens in him, which pushes him on to new creations. In reality, each writer writes only one book, each painter paints only one picture. Every new work is destined, in the mind of its author, to correct the preceding one, to complete the thought—which will not be completed. He does this work over and over again, wherever his sensation or thought was rendered imperfectly in the preceding work. When man interrogates and exerts himself, he does not really change. He only rids his nature of what is foreign to it, and deepens that portion that is his own. Those who burn their work before it is known, because it no longer satisfies them, are credited with great courage. I ask myself whether there is not still greater courage in admitting that one has not always been what one has become, in becoming what one is not yet, and in permitting to remain alive the material and irrefutable witnesses of the variations of one's mind.

I have, therefore, no more suppressed the *Introduction* of this volume than the chapters which follow it, where, however, ideas will also be found that I have great difficulty in recognizing to-day.[1] I cannot change the face that was mine ten years ago. And even if I could, should I exchange it for the one that is mine at the present day? I should lose, doubtless, for it is less young now. And who knows if one does not hate—just because one is older—the signs of youth in one's mind, as one disdains—because one regrets them—the remembrances of youth in one's body? In any case, hateful or not, one cannot modify the features of a face without at the same time destroying the harmony of the old face, and thereby compromising the features of the future face. For the greater part of the ideas which we think constitute

---

[1] The variants that I have introduced into this new edition—additions or subtractions—neither add to nor subtract anything from the general meaning of the work. They bear almost exclusively on the form.

PREFACE TO THE NEW EDITION

our present truth have as their origin precisely those which we believe constitute our past error. When we consider one of our early works, the passages which strike us the most are those which we love least. Soon we see no more than these; they fascinate us; they mask the entire work. On closing the book again they still pursue us; we ask ourselves why, and the result is—however little our courage—that we open roads for ourselves which we had not suspected. Thus it is that the critical spirit, made sharp and subtle by the disappointments and sufferings of one's intellectual development, becomes, little by little, the most precious, and doubtless the most active, auxiliary of the creative spirit itself.

I am a "self-taught" man. I confess it without shame and without pride. This first volume, which weighs on me, has served at least to inform me that if I was not yet, at the moment when I wrote it, out of the social herd, I was already repelled from entering the philosophic herd. The fact is that preconceived notions of æsthetics were so far from presiding over my education in art that it is my emotions as an artist which have led me, progressively, to a philosophy of art which becomes less and less dogmatic. In many of these old pages there will be found traces of a finalism which, I hope, has almost disappeared from my mind. The reason is that I have evolved with the forms of art themselves, and that, instead of imposing on the idols I adored *a* religion, I have asked these idols to teach me *religion*. All, in fact, revealed the same one to me, as well as the fact that

PREFACE TO THE NEW EDITION

it was quite impossible to fix it precisely, because it is universal.

I have had to make an effort in order to reach a harmonious conception of the plastic poem in which men commune. Even now it remains an undemonstrable, an intuitive, even a mystical, conception, if you like to call it that. Yet, in consideration of the effort expended, I hope that I may be pardoned the didactic solemnity of the beginning of my book. It is the mark of the thirtieth year, among those, at least, who have not the privilege of being free men at twenty and slaves at forty. When analysis begins to corrode one's early illusions, one draws oneself together, one wants to keep them intact, one defends oneself against the new illusions which are outlining themselves; one insists on remaining faithful to ideas and images, to means of expression that are no longer a part of one. One surrounds oneself with a hard mold which hampers one's movements. Is not that, in all æsthetic and moral evolutions of the past and the present, exactly the passage from the first instinctive ingenuousness to the free discovery of a second ingenuousness, exactly such a passage as we see in the stiffness of all archaisms? If I am not mistaken in this, I should be very well pleased if the tense character of the beginning of my book corresponded even a little to the tenseness of the first and most innocent among the builders of temples, the painters of tombs, and the sculptors of gods.

I have been reproached with having written not a "History of Art," but rather a sort of poem concern-

PREFACE TO THE NEW EDITION xxxix

ing the history of art. This reproach has left me wondering. I have asked myself what, outside of pure and simple chronology, the recital of inner events could be, when the material expression of those events consists entirely of affective elements. In the sense in which the historians understand history, synoptic tables suffice, and I have prepared them. There is no history except that summed up by these tables which is not, fatally, submitted to the interpretation of the historian.[1] What is true of the history of man's actions is infinitely more so of the history of his ideas, his sensations, and his desires. I cannot conceive a history of art otherwise than made up of a poetic transposition, not as exact, but as living as possible, of the plastic poem conceived by humanity. I have attempted that transposition. It is not my place to say whether I have succeeded with it.

To state the question a little differently, it seems to me that history should be understood as a symphony. The description of the gestures of men has no interest for us, no use, no sense even, if we do not try to seize on the profound relationships of these gestures, to show how they link together in a chain. We must try, especially, to restore their dynamic character, that unbroken germination of nascent forces engendered by the ceaseless play of the forces of the past on the forces of the present. Every man, every act, every work is a musician or an instrument in an orchestra. One cannot regard, it seems to me, the cymbal player or the triangle player as of the same importance as the

---

[1] Or rather, what history is there that the historian does not interpret?

violoncellos or of the mass of violins. The historian is the leader of the orchestra in that symphony which the multitudes compose with the collaboration of the artists, the philosophers, and the men of action. The historian's role is that of making clear the essential characters, to indicate their great lines, to make their volumes stand out, to contrast their lights with their shadows, to shade off the passages and harmonize the tones. It is so for the art-historian far more than for the historian of action—because the importance of action registers itself automatically in its results and traces, whereas the importance of a work of art is an affair of appreciation.

The historian should be partial. The historian who calls himself a scientist simply utters a piece of folly. I do not know, nor he either, any measuring instrument which shall permit him to graduate the respective importance of Leochares and Phidias, of Bernini and Michael Angelo. It seems that this is admitted with regard to literary history, and that no one thinks of getting wrought up if the historian of letters forgets Paul de Kock, voluntarily or not, to dilate upon Balzac. Neither is anyone surprised if the professor at the Sorbonne, writing a history of France, gives more importance to the gestures of Napoleon than to those of Clarke or Maret. The purists protest only when the partiality of sentiment intervenes to judge Napoleon, Clarke, or Maret. They do not realize that the mere statement of facts already supposes a choice made by men as a whole or by the events themselves, before the historian begins to intervene.

PREFACE TO THE NEW EDITION

When the question is one of contemporary history, the part of the orchestra leader is much more arduous to perform. The view of the facts as seen from a distance, the more or less strong or persistent influence of the events on minds, the memory that they have left, all these impose on him who writes a commentary of the past, certain summits, certain depressions, visible to all. And to recreate a living organism from them he need do no more than join them with a curve. From nearer by, intuition alone decides, and the courage to make use of it. So much the worse for him who does not dare and cannot leave to the future the task of saying whether he has done well or ill in dealing with the works and the men of his time, as an artist does with the light and shade which he distributes on the object. It is possible that, from the orthodox point of view of history, it is a heresy to affirm that the slightest study by Renoir, the slightest water color by Cézanne belongs much more effectively to the history of art than the hundred thousand canvases exhibited in ten years in all the *salons* of painting. And, notwithstanding, one must risk that heresy. The poet of the present makes the history of the future.

Let us go farther. The gesture of a hungry man who stretches out his hand, the words that a woman murmurs in the ear of the passer-by on some enervating evening, and the most infinitesimal human gesture have a much more important place in the history of art itself than the hundred thousand canvases in question, and the associations of interest which try to impose them on the public. The orchestral multitude brings into prominence the playing of artists like Cézanne and Renoir, and it is they, in turn, who make clear to us the value of the multitude, which is composed, only to an insignificant degree, of the mass of mediocre works. Amid them its voice arises like a cry in a silence full of indiscreet mimicry and excessive gesture. Our orchestra takes its elements from the widely scattered manners and customs, from the whole of their action on the evolution and exchange of ideas; it is in the discoveries, the needs, the social conflicts of the moment, the obscure and formidable upheavals that love and hunger provoke in the depths of collective life and the hidden springs of the individual conscience.

I am quite willing to mention even the movement called "artistic," which floats on the surface of history by means of institutes, schools, and official doctrines, like a rouge badly applied to a woman's face. It plays its little part in the great plastic symphony wherein Renoir and Cézanne in our time, for example, like Rubens and Rembrandt in another, play the most illustrious role. But it is only by indirect means that the spirit created in the crowds by this "artistic" movement, reacts on each new affirmation of a great artist—who is unaware of practically all its manifestations. I think that if the risk is greater for the modern historian who gives prominence to Cézanne and Renoir in his narrative, his attempt is as legitimate, from the "scientific" point of view as—for the historian of the past—the custom of quite candidly giving more importance to Phidias than to Leochares.

PREFACE TO THE NEW EDITION

The fact is that we have been for more than a century — since Winckelmann approximately — far too much inclined to tolerate a growing confusion between art history and archæology. One might as well confuse literature and grammar. It is one thing to describe, by their external character, the monuments that man has left on his journey, to measure them, to define their functions and style, to locate them in place and time—it is another thing to try to tell by what secret roots these monuments plunge to the heart of races, how they sum up the most essential desires of the races, how they form the recognizable testimony to the sufferings, the needs, the illusions, and the mirages which have hollowed out in the flesh of all men, living and dead, the bloody passage from sensation to mind. It is thus that in wanting to write a history that should not be a dry catalogue of the plastic works of man, but a passionate narrative of the meeting of his curiosity and education with the forms that lie in his path, I may have committed—I have committed—errors of archæology. Although I know worse errors, and although I have not failed to commit some of these besides, I will not go so far as to say that I do not regret them.

Archæology has been profoundly useful. By seeking and finding original sources, by establishing family likenesses, filiations, and the relationships of works and of schools, little by little, in the face of the diversity in the form of the images (from which so many warring schools of æsthetics have been inspired to create silly exclusivisms), archæology has defined the original analogy of these works and schools and the almost constant parallelism of their evolution. Everywhere, behind the artist, it has aided us to rediscover the man. Those among us, who have to-day become capable of entering into immediate communion with the most unexpected forms of art, evidently do not take note that such communion is the fruit of a long, previous education, for which archæology is doubtless the best preparation, however convinced of the fact it is itself. Those who rise up with the greatest contempt against the insensibility of the archæologist are probably those who owe him the greater part, if not of their sensibility, at least of the means which have permitted them to refine it. To-day we laugh at the worthy persons who grant scarcely a pitying look at the lofty spirituality of Egyptian statues, or who recoil in disgust before the grandiose bestiality of Hindu bas-reliefs. Notwithstanding, there were artists who *felt* like those same worthy persons. I should not affirm that Michael Angelo would not have shrugged his shoulders before an Egyptian colossus, and I am quite sure that Phidias would have thrown Rembrandt's canvases into the fire. Archæology, in plastics, is classification in zoölogy. Unknown to itself, it has fundamentally recreated the great inner unity of the universal forms and permitted the universal man to affirm himself in the domain of the mind. That this universal man will one day realize himself in the social realm is a thing I shall beware of maintaining, although it is a possible thing. But that some men, among the great diversity of the idols,

PREFACE TO THE NEW EDITION

can seize upon the one god who animates them all, is a thing as to which I may be permitted, I hope, to rejoice with them. Doubtless I shall even try soon to draw forth from the idols some of the features of this god.[1]

But not here. The scope is not broad enough. And I hope my reader is too impatient to approach the recital of the adventures which I have tried to relate for him, to consent to pick its flower before we have had the joy of breathing its perfume together. However, I should not like to have the slightest misunderstanding exist between him and me, as we stand at the threshold of this book. I have already warned him that I scarcely recognized myself in these opening pages of a work already old. They constitute, moreover, an obscure and often common plea for *the utility of art*. I want to dissipate the ambiguity. I have not ceased to think that art is useful. I have even strengthened my feeling as to that point. Not only is art useful, but it is, without the least doubt, the only thing that is, after bread, really useful to us all. Before bread, perhaps, for if we eat, it is really that we may keep up the flame which permits us to absorb —that we may recast it and spread it forth—the world of beneficent illusions which reveals itself and modifies itself, without a break, around us. From the caveman's or the lakeman's necklace of bones to the *image d'Epinal* tacked to the wall of the country tavern, from the silhouette of the aurochs dug in the wall of the grotto in Périgord to the ikon of the bed-

[1] *The Spirit of the Forms* (forthcoming).

room before which the muzhik keeps his lamp burning, from the war dance of the Sioux to the "Heroic Symphony," and from the graven design tinted with vermilion and emerald hidden in the night of the hypogees to the gigantic fresco which shines in splendor in the festival hall of Venetian palaces, the desire to arrest in a definite form the fugitive appearances wherein we think to find the law of our universe, as well as our own law, and through which we keep alive in ourselves energy, love, and effort—is manifested with a constancy and a continuity which have never abated. Whether this be in dance or song, whether it be in an image or in the narrative recited to a circle of auditors, it is always the pursuit of an inner idol—which we think, each time, to be the final pursuit and which we never end.

Philosophers, in speaking of this "disinterested play," affirm the irresistible need, which has urged us from the earliest times, to externalize the secret cadences of our spiritual rhythm in sounds or in words, in color or in form, in gesture or in steps. But the need asserts itself from this point of view as, on the contrary, the most universally interested of the deeper functions of the mind. Moreover, all games in themselves, even the most childish, are attempts to establish order in the chaos of confused sensations and sentiments. Man in his movement thinks that he adapts himself unceasingly to the surrounding world in its movement. And he believes that this adaptation takes place through the fleeting certitude he has of describing it forever in the intoxication of expression,

PREFACE TO THE NEW EDITION

as soon as he imagines that he has grasped a phenomenon as a whole. Thus, what is most useful to men is play.

The love of play, and the search for it, and the ardent curiosity which is a condition of play, create civilization. The civilizations—I should have said, those oases sown the length of time or dispersed in space, now alone, now interpenetrating, fusing at other times, attempting schemes, one after another, for a unanimous spiritual understanding among men —a possible, probable understanding, but one that is undoubtedly destined, if it be realized, to decline, to die, to seek within itself and around it the elements of a renewal. A civilization is a lyric phenomenon, and it is by the monuments which it raises and leaves after it that we appreciate its quality and its grandeur. It is defined to the extent that it imposes itself upon us through an impressive, living, coherent, and durable style. What men understand almost unanimously as "civilization" at the present hour has nothing at all to do with it. The tool of industry—the railroad, the machine, electricity, the telegraph—is only a tool. Whole peoples can employ it for immediate and materially interested purposes, without any opening up in them, by that employment, of the deep springs of attention and emotion, of the passion for understanding, and the gift for expressing which alone lead to the great æsthetic style wherein a race communes for a moment with the spirit of the universe. From this point of view the Egypt of five thousand years ago, the China of five centuries ago are more civilized than the America of to-day, whose style is still to be born. And the Japan of fifty years ago is more civilized than the Japan of to-day. It is even possible that Egypt, through the solidarity, the unity, and the disciplined variety of its artistic production, through the enormous duration and the sustained power of its effort, offers the spectacle of the greatest civilization that has yet appeared on the earth, and that all manifestations we call civilized since Egypt are only forms of dissolution and dissociation from her style. We should have to live ten thousand years more in order to know.

Style, in any case—that clear and harmonious curve which defines for us, on the road we follow, the lyrical steps established by those who preceded us, style—is but a momentary state of equilibrium. We cannot go beyond it. We can only replace it. It is the very negation of "progress," which is possible only in the realm of tools. Through the latter and in proportion to the number and the power of the means invented by man, "progress" increases the complexity of life and—by the same token—the elements of a new equilibrium. The moral order and the æsthetic order can, thanks to these tools, make up vaster symphonies, more mixed and complicated with influences and echoes, and served by a far greater number of instruments. But "moral progress," like "æsthetic progress," is merely bait which the social philosopher offers to the simple man in order to incite and increase his effort. Evil, error, ugliness, and folly will always, in the development of a new style, play their indispensable role as a real condition of imagination, of meditation, of idealism, and of faith. Art is a lightning flash of harmony that a people or a man conquers from the darkness and the chaos which precede him, follow him, necessarily surround him. And Prometheus is condemned to seize the fire only that he may light up for a second the living wound in his side and the calm of his brow.

ANCIENT ART

Vezere at Eyzies

Chapter I. BEFORE HISTORY

I

THE dust of bones, primitive weapons, coal, and buried wood—the old human as well as solar energy—come down to us tangled like roots in the fermentation of the dampness under the earth. The earth is the giver of life and the murderess, the diffused matter which drinks of death to nourish life. Living things are dissolved by her, dead things move in her. She wears down the stone, she gives it the golden pallor of ivory or of bone. Ivory and bone before they are devoured become rough as stone at her touch. The wrought flints have the appearance of big triangular teeth; the teeth of the engulfed monsters are like pulpy tubercles ready to sprout. The skulls, the vertebræ, and the turtle shells have the gentle and somber patina of the old sculptures with

ANCIENT ART

their quality of absoluteness. The primitive engravings resemble those fossil imprints which have revealed to us the nature of the shell formations, of the plants

AUSTRIA (Cavern of Willendorff). Statuette of a woman, olithic limestone (*Vienna*).

and the insects which have disappeared, of turbans, arborescences, ferns, elytra, and nerved leaves. A prehistoric museum is a petrified garden where the

BEFORE HISTORY

slow action of earth and water on the buried materials unifies the work of man and the work of the elements. Above lies the forest of the great deer—the open wings of the mind.[1]

The discomfiture which we experience on seeing our most ancient bones and implements mingled with a soil full of tiny roots and insects has something of the religious in it. It teaches us that our effort to extricate the rudimentary elements of a social harmony from animalism surpasses, in essential power, all our subsequent efforts to realize in the mind a superior harmony which, moreover, we shall not attain. There is no invention. The foundation of the human edifice is made of everyday discoveries, and its highest towers have been patiently built up from progressive generalizations. Man copied the form of his hunting

Chipped flint
(*Museum of Saint Germain*).

---

[1] The illustrating of this chapter having presented special difficulties, we offer our warmest thanks to Messrs. Capitan and Breuil, on one hand, and to the firm of Masson et Cie., on the other, without whom we should not have been able to carry through our task. The works of Abbé Breuil, most of all, constitute the basis which will henceforth be indispensable for the artistic illustrating of any book devoted to the prehistoric period. It is, thanks to his admirable pastels, that the troglodyte frescoes of Périgord and of Spain have been given back to us in what is most probably their original character.

and industrial implements from beaks, teeth, and claws; from fruits he borrowed their forms for his first pots. His awls and needles were at first thorns and fishbones; he grasped, in the overlapping scales of the fish, in the articulation and setting of bones, the idea of structure, of joints and levers. Here is the sole point of departure for the miracle of abstraction, for formulas wholly purified of all trace of experience, and for the highest ideal. And it is here that we must seek the measure at once of our humility and strength.

The weapon, the tool, the vase, and, in harsh climates, a coarse garment of skins—such are the first forms, foreign to his own substance, that primitive man fashions. He is surrounded by beasts of prey and is assailed constantly by the hostile elements of a still chaotic nature. He sees enemy forces in fire, in storms, in the slightest trembling of foliage or of water, in the seasons, even, and in day and night, until the seasons and day and night, with the beating of his arteries and the sound of his steps, have given him the sense of rhythm. Art is, in the beginning, a thing of immediate utility, like the first stammerings of speech; something to designate the objects which surround man, for him to imitate or modify in order that he may use them; man goes no farther. Art cannot yet be an instrument of philosophic generalization, since man could not know how to utilize it. But he forges that instrument, for he already abstracts from his surroundings some rudimentary laws which he applies to his own advantage.

The men and youths range the forests. Their

weapon is at first the knotty branch torn from the oak or the elm, the stone picked up from the ground. The women, with the old men and the children, remain hidden in the dwelling, an improvised halting place or grotto. From his first stumbling steps man comes to grips with an ideal—the fleeing beast which represents the immediate future of the tribe; the evening meal, devoured to make muscle for the hunters; milk for the mothers. Woman, on the contrary, has before her only the near and present reality—the meal to prepare; the child to nourish; the skin to be dried; later on, the fire that is to be tended. It is she, doubtless, who finds the first tool and the first pot; it is she who is the first workman. It is from her realistic and conservative role that human industry takes its beginnings. Perhaps she also assembles teeth and pebbles into necklaces, to draw attention to herself and to please. But her positivist destiny closes the horizon to her, and the first veritable artist is man. It is man, the explorer of plains and forests, the navigator of rivers, who comes forth from the caverns to study the constellations and the clouds; it is man, through his idealistic and revolutionary function, who is to take possession of the objects made by his companion, to turn them, little by little, into the instruments that express the world of abstractions which appears to him confusedly. Thus from the beginning the two great human forces realize that equilibrium which will never be destroyed; woman, the center of immediate life, who brings up the child and maintains the family in the tradition necessary to social unity; man, the focus of the life of the imagination, who plunges into the unexplored mystery to preserve society from death through his directing of it into the courses of unbroken evolution.

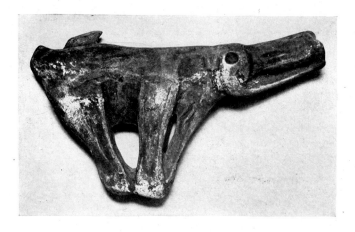

CAVERN OF BRUNIQUEL (Tarn-et-Garonne). Mammoth, carved reindeer horn (*Museum of Saint Germain*).

Masculine idealism, which later becomes a desire for moral conquest, is at first a desire for material conquest. For primitive man it is a question of killing animals in order to have meat, bones, and skins, and of charming a woman so as to perpetuate the species whose voice cries in his veins; it is a question of frightening the men of the neighboring tribe who want to carry off his mate or trespass on his hunting ground. To create, to pour forth his being, to invade surrounding life—in fact, all his impulses have their center in the reproductive instinct. It is his point of departure for all his greatest conquests,

BEFORE HISTORY

his future need for moral communion and his will to devise an instrument through which he may adapt himself intellectually to the law of his universe. He already has the weapon—the plate of flint; he needs the ornament that charms or terrifies—bird plumes in the knot of his hair, necklaces of claws or teeth, carved handles for his tools, tatooings, bright colors decorating his skin.

Art is born. One of the men of the tribe is skillful in cutting a form in a bone, or in painting on a torso a bird with open wings, a mammoth, a lion, or a flower. On his return from the hunt he picks up a piece of wood to give it the appearance of an animal, a bit of clay to press it into a figurine, a flat bone on which to engrave a silhouette. He enjoys seeing twenty rough and innocent faces bending over his work. He enjoys this work itself which creates an obscure understanding between the others and himself, between him and the infinite world of beings and of plants that he loves, because he is the life of that world. He obeys something more positive also—the need to set down certain acquisitions of primitive human science so that the whole of the tribe may profit by them. Words but inadequately describe to the old men, to the women gathered about, to the

SWITZERLAND (Kesslerloth). Reindeer grazing, engraved on reindeer horn (*Museum of Saint Germain*).

children especially, the form of a beast encountered in the woods who is either to be feared or hunted. The artist fixes its look and its form in a few summary strokes. Art is born.

II

The oldest humanity known, which defines our entire race, inhabited the innumerable grottos of the high Dordogne, near the rivers full of fish and flowing through reddish rocks and forests of a region once thrown into upheaval by volcanoes. That was the central hearth; but colonies swarmed the whole length of the banks of the Lot, of the Garonne, of the Ariège, and even to the two slopes of the Pyrenees and the

GROTTO OF CHAFFAUD (Vienne). Does, engraved bone (*Museum of Saint Germain*).

Cévennes. The earth was beginning to tremble less from the subterranean forces. Thickly growing green trees filled with their healthy roots the peat bogs that hid the great skeletons of the last chaotic monsters. The hardening of the crust of the earth, the rains and the winds that were regularized by the woods, the seasons with their increasingly regular rhythm, were introducing into nature a more apparent harmony. A suppler and more logical species, less submerged in primitive matter, had appeared little by little. If the cold waters, where the mammoth, the rhinoceros, and the lion of the caves came to drink, still harbored the hippopotamus, there were great numbers of horses, oxen, bison, wild goats, and aurochs living in the woods. The reindeer, the friend of the ice which descended from the Alps, the Pyrenees, and the Cévennes to the edge of the plains, lived there in numerous herds. Man had emerged from the beast in an overwhelming silence. He appeared about as he is to-day, with straight legs, short arms, a straight forehead, receding jaw, and a round and voluminous skull. By the action of the mind he is to introduce that harmony which was beginning to reign around him, into an imagined world which, little by little, would become his veritable reality and his reason for action.

The primitive evolution of his conception of art is, as we may naturally understand, extremely obscure. At such a distance everything seems on the same plane, and the divisions of time we establish are doubtless illusory. The paleolithic period ended with the quaternary age, at least twelve thousand years before us, and the art of the troglodytes, at that distant epoch, had already attained the summit of its curve. The development of a civilization is slow in proportion as it is primitive. The first steps are those that are the most uncertain. The millions of flaked axes found in the caverns and in the beds of rivers, the few thousands of designs engraved on bone or on reindeer horn, the carved hafts and the frescoes discovered on the walls of the grottos, evidently represent the production of a very long series of centuries. The variations of the images preserved cannot be explained only by the differences of individual temperaments. The art of the troglodytes is not made up of obscure gropings. It develops with a logic and an increasing intelligence about which we can only guess, and of which we can trace the great lines, but which we shall doubtless never be able to follow step by step.

What is sure is that the paleolithic artist belonged to a civilization that was already very old, one which sought to establish, through interpreting the aspects of the surroundings in which it was destined to live, the very law of these surroundings. Now no civilization, however advanced, has any other incentive or any other purpose. The reindeer hunter is not only the least limited of primitives, he is the first civilized man. He possessed art and fire.

In any case, the farther we descend with the geological strata into the civilizations of the caverns, the more it reveals itself as an organism coherent in its extent—from the Central Plateau to the Pyrenees—and coherent in its depth through its century-old traditions, its already ritualized customs, and its power of evolution in submission to the common law of strong, human societies. From layer to layer its set of tools improves, and its art, starting from the humblest industry and culminating in the moving frescoes of the grottos of Altamira, follows the logical incline that proceeds from the ingenuous imitation of the object to its conventional interpretation. First

CAVERN OF COMBARRELLES (Dordogne). Mammoth, scratched on interior wall (*Revue de l'Ecole d'Anthropologie*, 1902).

comes sculpture, the object represented through all its profiles, having a kind of second real existence; then the bas-relief, which sinks and effaces itself until it becomes engraving; finally the great pictorial convention, the object projected on a wall.[1]

This suffices for the rejection of the customary comparisons. The reindeer hunter is not a contemporary primitive, polar or equatorial; still less is he

---

[1] Thus it is that the Venus of Willendorff, the most ancient human form in sculpture that we know, is probably several decades of centuries earlier, despite its admirable character, than the works of Vézère and of Altamira.

14   ANCIENT ART

a child. The works that he has left us are superior to the greater part of the production of the Inoits, to all those of the Australians, and especially to those of children. The present-day primitive has not attained a stage so advanced, in his mental evolution. As to the child, he does nothing lasting; it is on sand or on scraps of paper that he traces his first lines, by chance, between other games. He has neither the

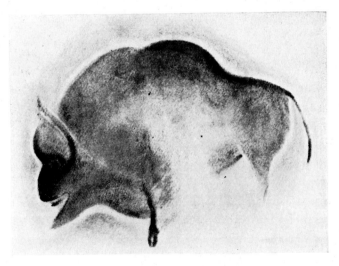

FOND DE GAUME (Dordogne). Bison, in polychrome, fresco; after the pastel by Abbé Breuil in *La Caverne du Fond de Gaume* (Capitan, Breuil, and Peyrony).

will nor the patience nor, above all, the deep need that must exist before he can imprint on one hard substance with another hard substance the image he has in his mind. James Sully [1] has very well shown this; the child adheres to an almost exclusively sym-

---
[1] James Sully, *Studies in Childhood*.

BEFORE HISTORY

bolic representation of nature, to a stammering series of ideographic signs which he changes at each new attempt; he has no care either for the relationships of the forms or for their proportions, or for the character of the object which he represents crudely, without

FOND DE GAUME (Dordogne). Reindeer grazing, fresco (*Revue de l'Ecole d'Anthropologie*, 1902); after a pastel by Abbé Breuil.

studying it, without even casting a glance at it if it is within range of his eye. It is probable that he draws only from a spirit of imitation, because he has seen people draw or because he has seen pictures and knows that the thing is possible. If he were not deformed by the abuse of conventional language which takes place around him, he would model before he painted.

Among the reindeer hunters, it is quite rare to find an image of entirely infantile character. In fact, such an image must be the work of a bad imitator who has seen an artist of his tribe carving or engraving.

Or else, as in the south of Spain, it belongs to a decadent school, later than the great period, of which Altamira is doubtless the highest manifestation. It then presents, like all decadences, a double character of puerility quite comparable to that of the stammering attempts of the negroes of South Africa, and of artistic refinement, where the ideographic scheme is visibly pursued. The real childhood of humanity has left us nothing, because it was incapable, like the childhood of a man, of continuity in effort. The art of the troglodytes of Périgord is not this impossible art of human childhood, but the necessary art of human youth, the first synthesis which the world, naïvely interrogated, imposes on the sensibility of a man, and which he gives back to the community. It is the synthetic intuition of the beginnings of the mind, which rejoins, across a hundred centuries of analysis, the generalizations of the most heroic geniuses, in the most civilized ages. Does not natural philosophy confirm the greater part of the presentiments of the mythological cosmogonies?

Where should he find the elements of this first synthesis if not in his own life? Now the life of the reindeer hunter is hunting and fishing. He characterizes it by his whole art—sculpture, bas-relief, engraving, and fresco. Everywhere we find wild animals and fish. From these, which are associated with all his earthly actions, he draws that profound love for animal form which makes his work resemble natural sculptures—bone-structures twisted by the play of muscles, beautiful skeletons sculptured by the

BEFORE HISTORY

atavistic powers of adaptation to function. All day long he sees these animals living, peaceful or hunted, grazing or fleeing; he sees the panting of their flanks, their jaws opening or shutting, their hair matted with blood or sweat, their skins wrinkled like trees or mossy like rocks. At evening, in his cavern, he skins the dead animals, he sees the bones appear under the torn flesh, the tendons shining on the hard surfaces; he studies the beautiful smooth vaults of the cavities and the heads of joints, the arch of the ribs, of the vertebræ, the round levers of the limbs, the thick armament of the pelvis and of the shoulder blades, the

FOND DE GAUME (Dordogne). Wolf, in polychrome, fresco; after the pastel by Abbé Breuil in *La Caverne du Fond de Gaume* (Capitan, Breuil and Peyrony).

jaws sown with teeth. His hand, which works in ivory and horn, is familiarized by touch with skeletons, sharp ridges, rough curves, silent and sustained planes; and it is the joy of his hand to feel the same projections and the same surfaces born of its own work. The artist, by great flakes, carves the handles of daggers, chisels the polished ivory into the forms of beasts, the mammoth with its four feet together, the reindeer, the wild goat, and skinned or living heads. Sometimes he even tries to rediscover in his material the forms of the woman he loves, of the female troglodyte whose haunches are broad, whose belly is covered with hair and broken down with maternity, whose warm flesh welcomes the fulfillment of his desire or lulls his fatigue.

Later, with the more rapid process of engraving, the field of exploration widens. The whole of the glacial fauna invades art. The mammoth, the cave bear, the bison, horse, aurochs, and especially the reindeer—the reindeer in repose or walking slowly, its head to the ground to crop the grass; the reindeer galloping, its nostrils to the wind, its horns on its back, fleeing before the hunter; sometimes the hunter himself, quite naked, hairy, armed with a spear and creeping toward the animal. Nothing surpasses the direct force of expression of some of these engravings. The line is drawn with a single stroke and bites deeply into the horn. The artist is often so sure of himself that he does not even join his lines, but merely indicates the direction of the principal ones which portray the attitude and mark the character. We see a horse's head made up simply of nostrils and jaws; the delicate legs of a reindeer with sharp hoofs, its horns spreading like seaweed or like great butterflies, sharp of breast and thin in the rump; hairy mammoths, on

BEFORE HISTORY

their massive feet, with vast curving spines, long trunk, small skull, and sharp little eyes; bison with their mountainous backs, their formidable neck and hard hocks; fighting beasts, running beasts, irresist-

FOND DE GAUME (Dordogne). Bison, fresco; after the pastel by Abbé Breuil (*Revue de l'Ecole d'Anthropologie*).

ible masses, wild flights under the branches—all the violent life of the hunter is evoked by these strong images, with their rude frame of rivers, great cool woods, grottos, dry days, and the cold scintillation of the night.

Never was a human society so thoroughly a part of its surroundings as the tribes of reindeer hunters. Hunting and fishing are at once the means and the purpose of life, and the rude existence is pursued even in the evening, in the cavern which forms part of the crust of the earth, and from which it was necessary to dislodge the lion and the bear. The tales of the hunters, the questions of the children, the work of the artists, the workmen in stone and in wood, the women, all tell the story of the forest and the water, from the skins and the furs stretched on the ground, from the implements of bone and ivory, the vegetable fibers, the beds of dry leaves, and the fagots of dead branches to the stalactites of the vault from which moisture drops. On winter evenings, the evenings of fires and legends, the dying or rekindling lights

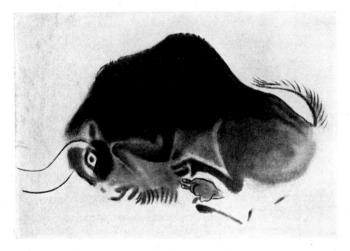

ALTAMIRA (Spain). Female bison, charging, fresco; after the pastel by Abbé Breuil in *La Caverne d'Altamira* (Cartailhac and Breuil).

sketch fleeting apparitions on the shadowy background. They are the dead beasts who return, the beasts to be killed who defy the hunter, those of whose meat the tribe has eaten so much, of whose bones it has wrought so much that they become protecting divinities for the tribe. From that time it was thought proper to set up their image in the most distant and dark corners of the cavern, whence their power would be increased by obscurity and mystery.[1] Fresco appears, broad synthetic paintings, ocherish, black, sulphurous, almost terrifying to behold in their shadows and through their unfathomable antiquity—reindeer and bison, horses and mammoths, sometimes composite monsters, men with the heads of animals. Sometimes, as at Altamira, we find all the beasts in a disordered troupe and, amid them, admirable figures that only a great artist could create, through definite, epitomized, purposeful drawing, through subtle modeling that undulates like watered silk, and through skillful transitions; the life of it is violent, the character is prodigious.

III

The fresco of the caverns is, therefore, the first visible trace, probably, of religion, which will henceforth pursue its course in common with art. It is born, like art, of the contact of sensation and of the world. At the beginning, everything, for the primitive, is natural, and the supernatural appears only with knowledge. Religion, thenceforward, is the miracle; it is what man does not know, has not yet attained, and later, what he wants to know and attain—his ideal. But before the coming of the supernatural, everything in nature explains itself because man lends to all forms, to all forces, his own

---
[1] Salomon Reinach, *L'Art et la Magie*.

will and his own desires. It is to attract him that the water murmurs, to frighten him that the thunder rolls, to awaken his anxiety that the wind makes the trees tremble, and the beast is, like himself, filled with intentions, with malice, with envy. So he must propitiate and adore its image, that it may let itself be captured and eaten. Religion does not create art; on the contrary, it is developed by art, and is planted triumphantly in the sensuality of man by giving a concrete reality to the happy or terrible images through which the universe appears to him. At base, what he adores in the image is his own power to render the abstraction concrete, and through it to increase his means of comprehension.

But religion is not always so docile. It sometimes revolts, and, to establish its supremacy, orders art to disappear. That is doubtless what happened in the Neolithic periods, sixty centuries perhaps after the waters of the deluge had engulfed the civilization of the reindeer. For a reason that is not yet well known, the air becomes warmer, the ice melts. The ocean currents doubtless modify their original course, western Europe grows warmer and the tepid water of the oceans, drawn up by the sun and carried by the winds towards the mountains, falls in torrents on the glaciers. Water streams through the valleys, the swollen rivers drown out the caverns, the decimated tribes flee from the disaster, follow the reindeer to the polar regions, or wander poverty-stricken and at random, driven from one resting place to another by the deluge or by hunger. With the daily struggle against elements too strong for them, with the dispersal of families, the loss of traditions and of implements, discouragement comes, then indifference and the decline toward the lower grades of animalism, which had so painfully been climbed. When the surroundings become more favorable, when the earth dries in the sun, when the

ALTAMIRA (Spain). Wild boar galloping, fresco; after the pastel by Abbé Breuil in *La Caverne d'Altamira* (Cartailhac and Breuil).

sky clears and the withdrawing of the glaciers permits the grass to grow green and flourish in the moraines, everything is to be re-established—the supply of tools, shelter, social relationships, and the slow, obscure ascent toward the light of the mind. Where are the reindeer hunters, the first conscious society? The prehistoric middle ages give no answer.

We must await another dawn to reveal the new humanity which has elaborated itself in the night.

It is, moreover, a paler dawn, chilled by a more positivist industry, a less powerful life; its religion is already turned from its natural source. The weapons and implements of stone that are found by millions in the mud of the lakes of Switzerland and eastern France, over which the re-established human tribes erected their houses to get shelter from hostile attacks, are now polished like the purest metal. Gray, black, or green; of all colors, of all sizes; axes, scrapers, knives, lances, and arrows — they have that profound elegance which always comes from close adaptation of the organ to the function which created it. The lake-dwelling society, which manufactured textiles and raised wheat, and was able to discover the ingenious system of dwellings built on piles, offers the first example of a civilization of predominantly scientific tendencies. The organization of life is certainly better regulated, more positive than in the ancient tribes of Vézère. But nothing appears of that ingenuous enthusiasm which urged the hunter of Périgord to recreate, for the joy of the senses and in the search for human communion, the beautiful moving forms among which he lived. There are, indeed, in the mud, among the polished stones, necklaces, bracelets, some potteries and numerous other witnesses to a very advanced industrial art, testifying to the economic

Pottery of the lake-men
(*Museum of Saint Germain*).

character of that society; but not a sculptured figure, not an engraved figure, not a bibelot which would lead us to believe that the man of the lakes had any presentiment of the common origin and vast solidarity of all the sensible forms which fill the universe.

Doubtless when men had retired to the cities on the lakes, the beneficent contact with the tree and with

Menhirs at Plouhermel (Morbihan).

the beasts of the forest occurred less frequently than in the days of the split stone; unquestionably men were less often inspired by the spectacle of the living play of animal forms. But there is, in the failure of these men to reproduce these forms, more than a sign of indifference. There is a mark of reprobation and probably of religious prohibition. Already at the same epoch there appear in Brittany and in England those somber battalions of stone, menhirs, dolmens, cromlechs, which have not told their secret, but which could scarcely signify anything else than an explosion of mysticism, a phenomenon which would be perfectly compatible, moreover—especially in a period of hard life—with the positivist activity which the daily struggle for bread and shelter necessitates. The double, the primitive form of the soul, has made its appearance behind the material phantom of beings

Dolmen at Erdeven (Morbihan).

and objects. From that time onward the spirit is everything, the form is to be disregarded, then condemned; first, because the dwelling of the evil spirit is seen in it, then—much later, at the dawn of the great ethical religions—because in it will be seen the permanent obstacle to moral liberation, which is, all things considered, the same thing. Even before the beginning of history, there appears, in groups of men, that need to destroy the equilibrium between our

BEFORE HISTORY

science and our desires, a need that is perhaps essential for the demolishing of a wearied society, in order that a field may be left free for newer races and conceptions.

However that may be, nothing that suggests the human form has been picked up under the dolmens, which also shelter flint axes and some jewels and—ten or twelve centuries before our era —the first metallic arms, helmets, and bucklers, bronze and iron swords. There is, indeed, in Aveyron, a sculptured menhir that represents, with extreme puerility, a female figure; there are, indeed, at Gavrinis, in Morbihan, on other menhirs, moving arabesques like the lines on the surface of low water, undulations or the tremblings of seaweed, which must be signs of conjuring or of magic. But, aside from these few exceptions, Celtic architecture remains mute. We shall never know what force it was that raised

NEOLITHIC AGE. Polished flint (*British Museum*).

these enormous tables of stone, erected these virile emblems to the sky, this whole hard army of silence which seems to have grown unaided from the soil, as if to reveal the circulation of the lava which makes the earth tremble.

With the last-raised stones ends the story of the prehistoric period in the Western world. Rome is coming to clear off the forests, bringing in its steps the Orient and Greece, dying Greece, and Assyria and Egypt already dead, after each had attained an incomparable summit. Such is the rhythm of history. On this soil, fifteen thousand years ago, lived a civilized society. It dies without leaving visible traces; five or six thousand years are needed for another rudiment of a social organism to be born in the same countries. But already, in the valley of the Nile, in the valleys of the Euphrates and the Tigris, a powerful human harvest has grown up, which flourishes for a moment, only to wither little by little. Athens mounts to the peak of history at the hour when the moors of Brittany were being covered with their dull flowers of stone; Rome comes to reap them; Rome goes down in the flood that rolls from the north; then the rhythm quickens—great peoples grow up on the cadavers of great peoples. In duration and in extent, history is like a boundless sea of which men are the surface and whose mass is made up of countries, climates, the revolutions of the globe, the great primitive springs, the obscure reactions of peoples, one on the other. When humanity shall begin to write its annals, the abysses will be filled up, the sea will seem quieter.

But perhaps this is nothing but illusion. A people is like a man. When he has disappeared nothing is left of him unless he has taken the precaution to leave his imprint on the stones of the road.

ART OF GAUL. The Gallic Hercules (*Museum of Aix*).

THE NILE

Chapter II. EGYPT

I

EGYPT is the first of those undulations which civilized societies make on the surface of history—undulations that seem to be born of nothingness and to return to nothingness after having reached a summit. She is the most distant of the defined forms which remain upon the horizon of the past. She is the true mother of men. But although her achievement resounded throughout the whole duration and extent of the ancient world, one might say that she has closed herself within the granite circle of a solitary destiny. It is like a motionless multitude, swelled with a silent clamor.

Egypt sinks without a cry into the sand, which has taken back, successively, her feet, her knees, her thighs, and her flanks, with only her breast and brow projecting. The sphinx has still, in his crushed visage, his inexorable eyes, outlined by rigid lids, which look inward as well as outward into the dis-

ANCIENT EMPIRE (XXX to XXV Century B.C.). Woman kneading (*Florence, Archæological Museum*).

tance, from elusive abstractions to the circular line where the curve of the globe sinks downward. To what depth do his foundations go, and how far around him and below him does history descend? He seems to have appeared with our first thoughts, to have followed our long effort with his mute meditation, to be destined to survive our last hope. We shall prevent the sand from covering him entirely because he is a part of our earth, because he belongs to the appearances amid which we have lived, as far back as our memories go. Together with the artificial mountains

EGYPT

with which we have sealed the desert near him, he is the only one of our works that seems as permanent as the circle of days, the alternation of the seasons, and the stupendous daily drama of the sky.

ANCIENT EMPIRE (xxx to xxv Century B.C.). The seated scribe (*Louvre*).

The immobility of this soil, of this people whose monotonous life makes up three-quarters of the adventure of humanity, seems to have demanded lines of

34 ANCIENT ART

stone to bind it, and these lines define the soil and the people even before we know their history. Everything around the pyramids endures. From the Cata-

ANCIENT EMPIRE (2500 B.C.?) Hawk's head, in gold (*Cairo Museum*). After an illustration in *Die Plastik der Ægypter* (published by Cassirer).

racts to the Delta, the Nile is alone between two identical banks, without a current, without a tributary, without an eddy, rolling on, from the depths of the centuries, its regular mass of water. Fields of barley, of wheat, of corn, palm trees, sycamores. A pitiless blue sky, from which the fire flows ceaselessly

ANCIENT EMPIRE (xxv Century B.C.?). Wooden statue, detail (*Museum of the Louvre*).

in sheets, almost dark during the hours of the day when the eye can look at it without difficulty, lighter at night when the rising tide of stars spreads its light there. Torrid winds rise from the sands. In the light, where the hot air vibrates, shadows are sharply outlined on the ground, and the unalterable colors—indigos, baked reds, and sulphurous yellows, turned to molten metal by twilights of flame, have only, as their transparent veil, the periodically changing green and gold of the cultivated land. A silence in which voices hesitate as if they feared to break crystal walls. Beyond these six hundred leagues of fixed and powerful life, the desert—without any other visible limit than the absolute circle which is also the horizon of the sea.

The desire felt there to seek and give form to eternity, imposes itself on the mind—the more despotically since nature retards death itself in its necessary acts of transformation and recasting. The granite is unbroken. Beneath the soil are petrified forests. In that dry air, wood that has been abandoned retains its living fibers for centuries, cadavers dry up without rotting. The inundation of the Nile, the master of the country, symbolizes, each year, perpetual resurrection. Its rise and fall are as regular as the apparent march of Osiris, the eternal sun, who arises each morning from the waters and disappears each evening in the sands. From the 10th of June to the 7th of October he pours on the calcined countryside the same fat, black mud, the mud which is the father of life.

The Egyptian people never ceased to contemplate

death. It offered the spectacle without precedent, and without another example to follow it, of a race intent for eighty centuries on arresting the movement of the universe. It believed that organized forms alone died, amid an immovable nature. It accepted the world of the senses only so long as it seemed to

MIDDLE EMPIRE (XVII Century). Scribes
(*Florence, Archæological Museum*).

endure. It pursued the persistence of life in its changes of aspect. It imagined alternate existences for itself. And the desire all men have to survive mortal death caused the Egyptians to endow the soul with that individual eternity of which the duration of cosmic phenomena gave them the vain appearance.

In their estimation man entered upon his true life at death. But, no less than in all the conceptions of immortality which succeeded theirs, did the desire of the Egyptians for immortality escape the irresistible need to assure a material envelope to the ever-living spirit. It was, therefore, necessary to construct a secret lodging, where the embalmed body should be sheltered from the elements, from beasts of prey, and especially from men. It must have with it its familiar objects—food and water; it was necessary above all that its image, the unchangeable envelope of the double which should not leave it again, should accompany it into the final shadow. And since nothing dies, it was necessary to shelter forever the symbolic divinities expressing the immutable laws and the resurrection of appearances—Osiris, fire, and the heavenly bodies, the Nile and the sacred animals which regulate the rhythm of their migration by the rhythm of its tides and its silences.

Egyptian art is religious and funerary. It began with the strangest collective madness in history. But since its poem to death lives, it touches the highest wisdom. The artist saved the philosopher. Temples, mountains raised by the hands of men, the Nile's own cliffs cut into sphinxes, into silent figures, dug out into labyrinthine hypogees, make a living alley of tombs to the river. All Egypt is there, even present-day Egypt which has required the most unchanging of the great modern religions; all Egypt, with its broken enigmas, its cadavers buried like treasures, perhaps a billion mummies lying in the darkness. And that Egypt which wanted to eternalize its soul with its bodily form is dead. The Egypt that does

MIDDLE EMPIRE (XVII Century B.C.). Colossus of Sowekhotep III (*Louvre*).

not die is the one which gave to stoneware, to granite, and to basalt the form of its mind. Thus the human soul perishes with its human envelope. But as soon as it is capable of cutting its imprint in an external material—stone, bronze, wood, the memory of generations, the paper which is recopied, the book which is reprinted and which transmits from century to century the heroic word and the songs—it acquires that relative immortality which endures so long as those forms shall endure in which our world has continued long enough to permit us to define it, and, through those forms, to define ourselves.

II

The temple, which sums up Egypt, has the categorical force of the primitive syntheses which knew no doubt, and by that very fact expressed the only truth we know as durable—that of instinctive life in its irresistible affirmation. Formed by the oasis, the Egyptian soul repeated the essential teachings of the oasis on the walls and in the columns of the temple. It shaped the granite of the temple into rectangular masses which rose in a block to the hard line of the angles, with the profile of the cliffs, with the straight-lined course of the river, with the hot sap that made the palm trees tower over the fields of emerald, of gold, and of vermilion. Dogma, which is a step, an ancient certitude confined within formulas open to our senses for the repose of our spirit, assumes invincible power when it is submitted for the adora-

EGYPT

tion of the multitudes in a garb in which they find again their true life, their familiar horizons, and the very material of the places where they pass their lives and whence their hope is born. The priest can make his house of the dogma, which the desire of men has materialized. He can insure his power by installing the god in the smallest, darkest, most secret retreat of the edifice. The worshiper will accept it, if he recognizes the visible face of his accustomed existence in the thousands of other mute gods that border the rigid avenues leading to the giant pylons, that people the courts and the porticos, and that are men mingled with the monsters of the oasis and the desert, lions, rams, jackals, cynocephali, and hawks. Amid the thick columns, laid low to-day by conquerors and covered by the waters and by sand, or still lifting the formidable discloated skeletons of the

MIDDLE EMPIRE (XVI Century B.C.). The bearer of offerings (*Louvre*).

hypo-style halls high above the desert, he will find himself. He will recognize his monotonous palm groves, his strange woods, his thickets with open spaces, the straight, thickset trunks of his trees with heavy crowns

NEW EMPIRE (XV Century B.C.). The herd, mural painting from Thebes (*British Museum*).

and opulent, pulpy fiber, crushed between the hardened mud of the ground and the vertical rays of the sun. The columns have the gathered thrust, the rough-grained roundness of the palm trees and the short, flattened surface of their tops. Leaves of lotus assembled into bouquets, leaves of the papyrus, palms, and rows of dates swell the capitals with the compact and powerful life of tropical vegetation. On looking beneath his feet he will see again the water lilies, the lotus, the heavy plants, the flora of the fecund river where moor hens and ducks thrive, as well as fish and crocodiles; he will perceive the lizards, the snakes, the uræus that warms itself on the hot sand where the red-brown elytra of the scarabs sow bits of metal. And when he raises his eyes it will be to divine, below the familiar constellations that sow the blue space, the birds of the solitudes, the slender

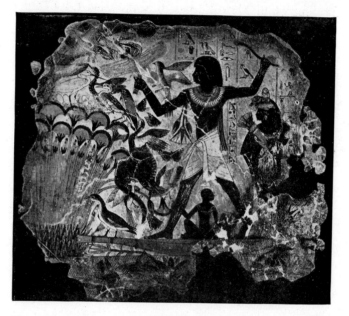

NEW EMPIRE (xv Century B.C.). The birds, mural painting from Thebes (*British Museum*).

ibis, the vulture, the symbolic hawk suspended on rigid wings between the sky and the desert. Everywhere, on the heights of walls, columns, obelisks, everywhere—living script will flower for the joy of his senses, in painted bas-relief, in hieroglyphic inscriptions. Its opaque emeralds and its somber turquoises, its burnt reds, its sulphur, and its gold will repeat to him the science, the literature, and the history which his ancestors were so long in making with their blood, their bones, their love, their memory, and the fearful or charming forms which accompanied them.

Entrenched behind this formal language, the priest may surround his action with a mystery by which he

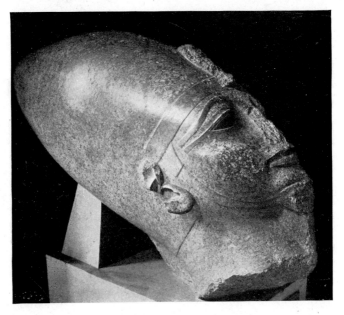

NEW EMPIRE (xv Century B.C.) Colossal head of Amenothes III (*Louvre*).

profits. He knows much. He knows the movements of the heavens. He arranges his temple as an observatory, protected by lightning conductors. He possesses the great principles of geometry and triangulation. But his science is secret. All that these people know of it is revealed by certain tricks of

EGYPT

spiritualism and of magic which mask the sometimes puerile and often profound meaning of the occult philosophy which the hieroglyphs and the symbolic figures are meant to eternalize on the face of the desert.

The Pharaoh, the human form of Osiris, is the instrument of the theocratic caste—which overwhelms him with power so as to domesticate him. Below it and him, with some intermediaries, officers, chiefs of cities or of villages, governors armed with their batons, is the multitude. For a few hours of repose in the burning night, on the ground of hardened mud, for bread and water, they have nothing but the life of the enslaved plowman or reaper, mason or stonecutter—forced labor and blows. A hundred generations are used up to build the pyramids, men are broken at tasks beyond the strength of man, women are deformed before their age because they have been too miserable and have borne too many children, children are turned aside and warped before birth under the weight of a servitude centuries old. A frightful nightmare. In the far background there is the bare hope of future metamorphoses, a troubled and flickering light for the poor man who will have no tomb.

New Empire. Hawk (*Louvre*).

How is it that, in this hell, the Egyptian did not seek and find the dangerous consolation of absolute spiritualism? The living desire is stronger than death. Naturalistic and polytheistic from its origin, his religion retained the love of the form upon which we base our hope. His statues gave to mystery an indestructible skeleton, and he never adored his gods save under animal or human forms. The surroundings in which he had to live did not permit him to become absorbed in unrestrained contemplation. The daily struggle for bread is the surest of positivist educations. As a matter of fact, nature is ungrateful in Egypt. It is only by incessant effort and thanks to resources constantly renewed, in their ingenuity and courage, that the Egyptian learned to utilize to his profit the periodical excesses of the Nile. He had to put into practice a study, centuries old, of the habits of the river, of the consistency and the qualities of the mud; he had to undertake formidable works, dikes, embankments, artificial lakes, irrigating canals, the cutting of sandstone and of granite; he had to continue these works ceaselessly and begin them again to prevent them from being buried under the deposits of the river, from being swallowed up and disappearing. The pyramids reveal the incomparable power of his engineers. And if the hardness of his life turned his mind toward death, at least during his passage over the earth he left the impress of a profound genius for geometry.

A strange people, expressing, in theorems of basalt, the most vast, the most secret, the most vague aspira-

EGYPT

tions of its inner world! The spirit of Egypt is absolute and somnolent like the colossuses stretched out on the stone of its tombs. And yet, outside of the mystery of ever-renewing life, forever like itself in all epochs, under all skies, there is nothing that is not

NEW EMPIRE. Ibis, bronze statuette (*Louvre*).

human and accessible to our emotion in the radiant silence which seems to well up from these motionless figures with their definite planes. The Egyptian artist is a workman, a slave who works under the baton like the others; he is not initiated into the mystic sciences. We know a thousand names of kings, of priests, of war chiefs, and of city chiefs; we do not know one name of those who have expressed the real thought of Egypt, that which lives forever in the stone of the tombs. Art was the anonymous voice, the mute voice of the crowd, ground down and observing within itself the tremor of the mind and of hope. Sustained by an irresistible sentiment of the life it was forbidden to spread out, it allowed that sentiment to burn—with all the power of its compressed faith—into depth.

It is not true—startling and illuminating as are the metaphysical intuitions that, with their power, the priestly castes pass on through time, in Egypt as in Chaldea—it is not true that the mysterious images which symbolize these intuitions owe to them their beauty. With the artist, instinct is at the beginning of everything. It is life, in its prodigious movement wherein matter and mind merge without his thinking of disuniting them, that lights the spark in him and directs his hand. It is for us to disengage from the work of art its general signification as we disengage it from sensuous, social, and moral life, which it sums up for us in a flash. The Egyptian artist followed certain ideas, more often restrictive than active, which the priest dictated to him. When the priest demanded that a lion with a human head be cut in granite, or a man with the head of an eagle and open hands through which the flame of the spirit seemed to pass into the world, he jealously kept to himself the occult meaning of the form and the gestures, and the sculptor drew the enthusiasm which made the material quiver from the material alone and from the faith he had in

New Empire (xiv Century B.C.). Sekhmet (*Louvre.*)

the myths he animated. If the monster was beautiful, it was because the sculptor was living. The profound occultist counted for nothing in it, the naive artist for everything.

We know really only what we have learned by ourselves, and personal discovery is our sole source of enthusiasm. The highest generalizations have started with the most obscure and strongest sentiment, to purify themselves step by step as they rise to intelligence. They are open to the artist who must, logically and fatally, take his course toward them. But the faculty of giving life to the language in which philosophers communicate these generalizations to us is not logically and fatally imparted to the intellectual. The generalization is never a point of departure, it is a tendency; and if the artist had begun with occultism, his work would have been condemned to the stiffness of death. Now, even when stiff as a cadaver, by the will of the priest, the Egyptian statue lives through the love of the sculptor. Only human evolution proceeds in a block, and the instinct of the artist accords with the mind of the philosopher in order to give to their abstract or concrete creations the same rhythm which expresses a general need felt in common.

III

However that may be, it was the crowd and nothing but the crowd which spread over the wood of the sarcophagi and over the compact tissue of the hypogees, the pure, living, colorful flowers of its soul. It whis-

EGYPT

pered its life in the deep shadows so that that life should shine in the light of our torches when we open the hidden sepulchers. The fine tomb was dug out for the king or the rich man, it is true, and his was the luxurious existence to be traced on the walls, in funeral

NEW EMPIRE.   Great temple of Thebes.

processions, in adventures of war or of hunting or in the work of the fields. He was to be shown surrounded by his slaves, by his farm workers, by his familiar animals; it was necessary to tell how his bread was made, how his beasts were cut up by the butcher, how his fish were caught, how his birds were captured, how his fruits were offered him, and how his wives made their toilet. And the crowd of artisans worked in obscurity; they thought to tell the charm, the power, the happiness, the opulence, and the life of the master;

they told, above all, their misery, but also their fecund activity, utility, intelligence, inner wealth, and the furtive grace of their own life.

What marvelous painting! It is freer than the statuary, which is intended almost solely to render the image of the god or the deceased. Despite its abstract grand style it is familiar, it is intimate; sometimes it turns to caricature; always it is malicious or tender, like this naturally human and good people, which is crushed little by little by theocratic force, and which descends into itself to consider its humble life. In the modern sense of the word there is no science of composition, no sense of perspective. Egyptian drawing is a writing that must be learned. But let one know it well, with its silhouettes whose heads and legs are always in profile while their shoulders and breasts are always in front view, and then see how all these stiff silhouettes move, with what ingenuousness they live, how their silence is peopled with animation and murmur! An extremely well-organized plan, sure, decisive, precise, but quivering. When the form appears, especially the nude form, or as it is divined through a transparent shirt, the artist suspends his whole life in it, that nothing but a light of the spirit may shine from his heart, one which shall illumine only the highest summits of memory and of sensation. Truly, that continuous contour, that single undulating line, so pure, so nobly sensual, which evinces so discreet and strong a sense of character, of mass, and of movement, has the appearance of being traced in the granite by the intelligence alone, without

New Empire (xiv Century B.C.). Portrait of a woman (*Florence, Archæological Museum*).

the help of a tool. Then come streaming the deep blues, emeralds, ochres, golden yellows, and vermilions —lightly, never thickly applied. It is like perfectly

NEW EMPIRE (XIV Century B.C.). A princess, stone (*Berlin Museum*). After an illustration in *Die Plastik der Ægypter*.

clear water into which one would let fall, without stirring it by a tremor, unchangeable colors: they do not muddy it, but let the plants and pebbles at the bottom be seen.

NEW EMPIRE. Temple of Touthmes III at Karnak.

The intensity of the sentiment, the logic of the structure break the chains of hieratism and the impulse to style. These trees, these stiff flowers, this whole conventional world has the heavy movement of the fruitful seasons, of the seed as it returns to life. Egyptian art is perhaps the most impersonal that exists. The artist effaces himself. But he has such an innate sense of life, a sense so directly moved and so limpid that everything of life which he describes seems defined by that sense, to issue from the natural gesture, from the exact attitude, in which one no longer sees stiffness. His impersonality resembles that of the grasses which tremble at the level of the ground or of the trees bowing in the wind with a single movement and without resistance, or that of the water which wrinkles into equal circles all moving in the same direction. The artist is a plant that gives fruits similar to those of other plants, and as full of savor and of nourishment. And the convention which dogma imposes upon him is not apparent, because that which issues from his being is animated by the very life of his being, healthy and swelling with juice as a product of the soil.

What he recounts is his life itself. The workmen with their tanned skin, their muscular shoulders, nervous arms, and hard skulls work wholeheartedly, even when the rod is used; their faces remain gentle —the smooth-shaven faces with the prominent cheeks; and it is not without a kind of fraternal irony that the artisan decorator or statue maker, who has represented himself so often, shows them busy at their task, rowers sweating, butchers cutting and sawing, masons assembling bricks of baked mud, herdsmen leading their passive beasts or delivering the females, fishermen, hunters, jovial farmhands holding up frantic ducks

New Empire (xiii Century B.C.). Temple of Ibsamboul.

by the tips of their wings and squirming rabbits by their ears, cramming fat geese, carrying cranes in their arms and holding their beaks closed with a firm fist so as to prevent them from screaming. We see the rearing of the heads, the ambling or mincing gaits, hear the bleating, the bellowing, and the sound of wings. The domestic animals—the oxen, asses, dogs, and cats—have their massive or peaceful or joyous or supple look, their unceasing rumination, the tremor of the skin or of their ears, their undulation as they creep, and the silence and surety with which they stretch their paws. The panthers walk as if on velvet, pushing out their flat heads. The ducks and geese waddle, digging and quacking with their flat bills. The stupid fish gape in the drawn nets; the trembling water is transparent, and the women who come to dip it up in their jars or the animals who plunge into it are saturated with its coolness. Oranges and dates have their weight in baskets which are held up by arms as pure as the stem of a young plant, and which are balanced like flowers. The women, when they bedeck themselves or moisten their slim brushes to rouge their mistresses, have the air of reeds bending down to the dew in the grass. The world has the silent shudder of the morning.

This natural poetry, fundamentally ardent and familiar, is carried by the Egyptians into everything that comes from their fingers—into their jewels, their little intimate sculpture, those innumerable knick-knacks which encumber their sepulchers, where they follow the dead person to whom they had belonged. And it is in the domestic objects of the kitchen and the workshop. All their fauna, all their flora live again there with that same very sensual and very chaste sentiment; all is motionless and alive; and all has the same profundity. Whatever their material—bronze or wood, ivory, gold, silver, or granite—they preserved, in the matter wrought, its weight and its delicacy, its freshness if of the vegetable world, its grain if a mineral. Their spoons resemble leaves abandoned at the water's edge; their jewels, cut into

New Empire (xiv Century B.C.). Hypostyle Hall of Karnak.

the shapes of hawks, reptiles, and scarabs, have the look of those colored stones that one picks up in the bed of rivers, on the seashore and in the neighborhood of volcanoes. Underground Egypt is a strange mine. It breeds living fossils which are like the crystallization of organic multitudes.

IV

But all the intimacy, all the furtive charm of its spirit is hidden there, like the fellah in his mud warren, far from the palaces and the temples. On the surface of the soil we get the philosophic Egypt. Only under the Ancient Empire, five or six thousand years ago, the Memphite school of sculpture essayed an expression of every-day existence. Egypt remembered old epochs of liberty, perhaps, before the sphinx himself, epochs of which we shall some day find traces under ten thousand years of alluvial deposits, lower than the foundations of the pyramids. Art, moreover, is always realistic at its beginnings. It does not yet know how to form those synthetic images, made up of the thousands of forms encountered on the long ascending road toward civilization, which art tries to realize as soon as it gets to the threshold of the general idea. Primitive man is almost solely concerned with his own life. Certainly he makes his attempt at résumés of sensations, but at résumés of things before his eyes, not of those which pass beyond the vision of the moment. It is in order to characterize well visible forms that he leaves nothing of them

EGYPT

but the summits of their undulations and of their expressive projections. The "Seated Scribe," which is of that ancient epoch, is of a terrifying truthfulness, in the man's direct application to the task he accom-

New Empire (XIII Century). Sarcophagus of Rameses III, detail (*Louvre*).

plishes. He is not yet a type of average humanity; he is already the average type of a profession and a caste. His attention to his work, his suspended energy, that arrested life which makes his face flame like a torch and that animates his fixed body are due to the planes which define him, and to the trenchant mind, free of disquietude, of the man who cut them. Of the same period are the peasants who march stick in hand, the men and women who start, side by side on the voyage of death, as they embarked on the voyage of life.

The Egyptian of that time possessed the equilibrium of his functions. Each wheel of the social machine acted, at that moment, with a vigor and an automatism which marked a life that was spontaneously disciplined, but free to define itself.

The classic sculpture came into existence only under the Middle Empire when Thebes had dethroned Memphis. From that moment and until the end of the world of the Nile, it was scarcely more than funerary and religious: statues of gods and statues of doubles. The story of the harvest, of the active work of the men and animals of the plow, of boudoir and household cares, of the adventures of every-day life, was left to painting and to the workmen of art. The sculptor of the gods was indeed a workman too, but he was raised, by the importance of his task and the strength of his faith, well above his misery. One might say that he had turned his back on the oasis, that he contemplated only the regularity of the days and the years, the sleeping and the awakening of the seasons, of the river, the sad desert, the impassible face of the sky.

We must not be too greatly surprised at seeing him thus different from the man who gave that account

EGYPT

of the scribe with so much passionate attention. From afar, Egyptian art seems changeless and forever like itself. From near by, it offers, like that of all the other peoples, the spectacle of great evolutions, of progress toward freedom of expression, of researches in imposed hieratism. Egypt is so far from us that it all seems on the same plane. One forgets that there are fifteen or twenty centuries, the age of Christianity— between the "Seated Scribe" and the great classic period, twenty-five or thirty centuries, fifty, perhaps — twice the time that separates us from Pericles and Phidias—between the pyramids and the Saite school, the last living manifestation of the Egyptial ideal.

NEW EMPIRE. Woman seated, bronze statuette (*Louvre*).

The arresting of Egyptian sculpture in the movement of free discovery, sketched with so much vigor by the Memphite school, was doubtless provoked by a long historical preparation whose elements are too little known for us to define them with sufficient precision. The Ancient Empire was peaceful. The Theban Empire is warlike. It draws its authority more directly from the priestly caste, in order to retain the obedience of the industrious and gentle people whom it wanted to use in its ambition for conquest. The theological mystery becomes denser. Dogma, growing more fixed, limits the flight of sculpture and, by imposing limits upon it, condemns it to research of a restricted type, which will narrow it more and more. It becomes the religious expression of a people of engineers. The statues will define the permanent aspect of Egypt, arrest life between regular dikes, cause the world to begin and end with them as the cultivated land ends and the desert begins with the limit of the river mud. Egyptian sculpture becomes a changeless architectonic frame; a century-old study of form, having penetrated the laws of its structure, has affixed this frame which will henceforth enclose the portrait of the god or the portrait of the deceased, the dwelling place of the double. Everything changes. Forms are born and effaced on the surface of the earth as easily as figures on a blackboard. There is nothing changeless save the almost mathematical relationships which animate them, binding them together with the invisible chain of abstraction. The great sculpture of Egypt materializes that abstraction and formulates in granite a geometrical ideal that seems as durable as the laws which govern the course of the heavenly bodies and the rhythm of the seasons.

Sculpture is at once the most abstract and the most positive of plastic expressions—positive, because it is impossible to evade the difficulties of the task through verbal artifices and because the form will live only on condition that it be logically constructed, from whatever side one considers it; abstract, because the law of that construction is revealed to us only by a series of more and more generalized mental operations.

NEW EMPIRE. Spoons for rouge (*Louvre*).

Before it was an art, sculpture was a science, and no sculptor can produce durable work if he has not found the generating elements of it in Nature herself. Now it was the Egyptians who taught us that, and it is perhaps not possible to understand and to love sculpture if one has not first undergone the severe education they afford us.

The head of their statues remains a portrait, to which style is given by the subordination of its characteristics to a few decisive planes, but the body is molded in a canon of architectural science which will not be reached again. One foot is in front of the other or beside it; the statue, almost always crowned with the pschent, is half nude, standing with the arms glued to the sides or seated, the elbows at the thorax, the hands on the knees, the face looking straight ahead, the eyes fixed. It is forbidden to open its lips, forbidden to make a gesture, forbidden to turn its head, to arise, to leave its pedestal in order to mingle with living beings. One would say that it was tied down with bands. But yet it bears within it, in its visage, where thought wanders with the light, and in its immobilized body, the whole life spread out on the walls of the tombs, the bursting life of the shadows. A wave runs through it, a subterranean wave, whose sound is stifled. The statue's profiles have the sureness of an equation of stone and a sentiment so vast that everything of which we are in ignorance seems to reside in it silently. It will never tell its secret. The priest has enchained its arms and its legs, sewn up its mouth with mystic formulas. Egypt will not attain the philosophic equilibrium—that sense of the relative which gives us the sense of the measure of our action and, in revealing to us our true relationships with things in their ensemble, assigns

EGYPT

to us, in the harmony of the universe, the role of conscious center of the order which it imposes on us. She will not know the freedom toward which she was tending in the period of Memphis, and which the painters suspect as they grope about in the darkness of the tombs. The priest forbids her to demand of the confused movement of nature an agreement between his science and the aspirations of sentiment which she can not repress and which shine from the basalt as from an arrested sun.

Master of the soul, or at least holding by the wrist the hand that expresses it, the priest permits all things to the king, who permits all things to the priest. From the beginning of the Middle Empire to the end of the New, Egypt returns to the spirit that erected the pyramids. She will cover herself with giant temples and with colossuses, Ibsamboul, Luxor, Karnak, Ramesseum, Memnon, piles of stone, walls, pylons,

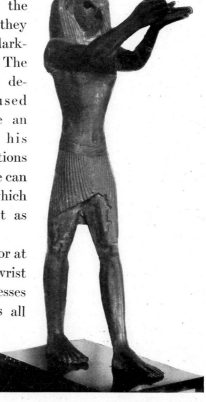

SAITE EPOCH. Horus, bronze (*Louvre*).

statues of disproportionate size, sphinxes, mill wheels of stone under which the king in his pride grinds the multitude which, in turn, is consoled by its pride in making gods. At this moment everything is possible to the sculptor-geometer. One does not know whether he cuts the rocks into colossuses or whether he gives to the colossuses the appearance of rocks. He penetrates into hills of granite, scoops out immense halls there, covers them from top to bottom with immense bas-reliefs and painted hieroglyphs, gives their front which faces the Nile the aspect of giant figures as decisive as the first profiles he traced—figures whose great pure faces stare, for three or four thousand years without the turn of an eyelid, at the terrible sun, which sculptures them with absolute shadows and lights. The monsters he erects as the borders of avenues, the monsters which tell nothing and reveal everything, are rigorously logical, despite their man's or ram's head on a lion's body. That head is attached naturally to the shoulders, the muscles barely indicated have their normal insertions and direction, the bones their necessary architecture, and from the tips of the claws and the silent planes of the sides, from the rump and the back to the round cranium and to the meditative face, the vital forces circulate with one continuous flow. When the artist cuts straight from the block these absolute forms whose surfaces seem determined by geometrical volumes penetrating one another according to immutable laws of attraction, one would say that he retains, in the depth of his inexhaustible instinct, the remembrance of the common form from

EGYPT

which all others come: animal forms, and, beyond the animal forms, those of the original sphere whence the planets issued and whose curve was sculptured by the gravitation of the heavens. The artist has the right to create monsters if he can make of them beings which can conceivably live. Any form adapted to the universal conditions of life is more living, even if it exists only in our imagination, than a form based on reality but fulfilling its function badly. The dried-out cadavers, which the soil of Egypt will finally absorb bit by bit, have not the reality of her sphinxes and her fearful gods with men's bodies and the head of hawks and panthers, where the spirit has laid its spark. In all directions and from whatever point one considers them, they undulate like a wave. One would say that an insensible line of light turns about them, slowly caresses an invisible form which its embrace reveals, itself searching out the place—without the intervention of the sculptor—where it is to be inflected or where it is to insinuate itself, barely to modulate the undulating

SAITE EPOCH (670 B.C.). Doll, wood (*British Museum*).

progression of the sculpture by imperceptible passages, as music does.

But this definitive science will eventually destroy the statue maker's art. An hour arrives when the mind, directed along a single road, can discover nothing more there. Doubtless the immobility of Egypt had never been more than an appearance. But the ideal of her mind, even if she tried to define herself in new forms, changed but little, for the teachings of her soil scarcely varied and it was always with the same surroundings that man had to reckon. And she had expended a prolonged effort to approach that ideal. It was for this reason that she had not died. She struggled. But the Theban empire was immobile. The dogma no longer moved; the social order had been poured into its granite mold which the monarchy sealed. Enthusiasm wears itself out if it recommences the same conquests every day. Under the Ramessides, the overstrained effort of the preceding dynasties was disunited. Continual war with outside powers, invasions, and foreign influences discouraged and unsettled the spirit of the Egyptians. After fifteen centuries of uninterrupted production, the Theban statue maker handled his material with too great facility. Occultism was, however, cultivated as much by the priestly classes and was thus the master that directed the artisan. But he had lost the power of action. He had lost that prodigious sense of mass that concentrates life in a decisive form of which all the surfaces seem to rejoin the infinite through their unlimited curves. Each year he delivered by hundreds

EGYPT

statues manufactured in quantity from the same commercial model. The school was formed. Geometrical idealism had fixed itself in a formula and sentiment had exhausted itself through continually encountering those unscalable walls of stone which forbade it to go farther. Egypt died of her need of eternity.

V

But her death was to be a slow one. She was even to have, before passing on the torch to younger hands, a fine reawakening to action. With the Saite dynasty, about the time when Greece emerged from the myth into history, she profited by the decadence of Assyria and that of the interior organization of the Medo-Persian power, to recover courage, in view of her re-established security. Once more she looked about her and into herself, and discovered in her old soul—infused with freshness by the confused presentiment of a new ideal—a supreme flower, as warm as an autumn. She cradled

SAITE EPOCH. Queen Karomana, bronze statuette (*Louvre*).

nascent Greece with a farewell song, still quite virile, and very gentle.

Saite art returned to original sources. It was as direct as the ancient Memphite art. But it has almost rediscovered the science of Thebes, and if it seems softer than Theban art, it is because its tenderness is more active. Now, we no longer find only funerary statues. Saite art escapes the formula; it produces faithful portraits, precise and nervous—scribes again, statuettes of women, personages seated on the ground, their hands crossed on their knees, at the height of the chin.

Egypt did not fail to obey that consoling law which decrees that every society about to die from exhaustion or which feels itself dragged into the current of revolution, shall turn back for a moment to address a melancholy farewell to woman, to her indestructible power which society, in the course of its vigorous youth, has usually misunderstood. Societies rising in full flight are too idealistic, too much concerned with the conquest and the assimilation of the universe, to look in the direction of the hearth they are abandoning. It is only on the other slope of life that they look backward to bow their wiser or more discouraged enthusiasm before the force that conserves while everything around it wearies, droops and dies—beliefs, illusions which are presentiments, and civilizing energy. Egypt at her decline caressed the body of woman with that sort of chaste passion which only Greece knew afterward, and which Greece perhaps did not express so religiously. Feminine forms, sheathed in

SAITE EPOCH (VI Century B.C.). Seated personage, bronze (*Louvre*).

a clinging material, have that pure lyrism of young plants that reach up to drink the daylight. The silent passage from the slim round arms to the shoulders, to the ripening breast, to the waist, to the belly, to the long, tapering legs, and to the narrow, bare feet has the freshness and the quivering firmness of flowers not

PTOLEMAIC EMPIRE (I Century B.C.). Temple of Denderah.

yet opened. The caress of the chisel passes and slips over the forms like lips brushing a closed corolla which they would not dare to press. Man, grown tender, gives himself to her whom till then he had thought only to take.

In these last works Egypt confides to us her most intimate thought about the young women and the men seated like the boundary marks of roads. Everything is a restrained caress, a veiled desire to penetrate universal life before Egypt abandoned herself unresistingly to its current. As a musician hears harmony, the sculptor sees the fluid of light and shade that makes the continuous world by passing from one form to another. Discreetly he joins the projections that are barely indicated by the long, rhythmic planes of the thin garment which has not a single fold. The model-

Ptolemaic Empire (i Century B.C.). Temple of Denderah, bas-relief.

ing passes like water, over the most compact materials. Its wave flows between the absolute lines of a geometry in movement, it has the balanced undulations that one would call eternal, like the movement of the sea. Space continues the block of basalt or of bronze by taking up from its surface the confused illumination that arises from its depths. The mind of dying Egypt tries to gather together the general energy dispersed through the universe, that it may transmit it to men to come.

And that is all. The walls of stone that inclosed the soul of Egypt are broken by invasion, which recommences and finds her at the end of her strength. Her whole inner life runs out of the open wound. Cambyses may overturn her colossuses; Egypt cannot offer a virile protest; her revolts are only on the surface and accentuate her decline. When the Macedonian comes, she willingly includes him among her gods, and the oracle of Ammon finds it easy to promise him victory. In the brilliant Alexandrian epoch her personal effort was practically *nil*. It was the Greek sages and the apostles of Judea who came to drink at her spring, now almost dried up, but still full of deep mirages, that they might try, in the unsettled world, to forge from the debris of the old religions and the old sciences a new weapon for the idea. She saw, with an indifferent eye, the dilettante from Hellas visiting and describing her monuments, and the Roman parvenu raising them again. She let the sand mount up around the temples, the mud fill the canals and bury the dikes, and the weariness of life slowly covered up her heart. She did not disclose the true depth of her soul. She had lived inclosed, she remained inclosed, shut like her coffins, her temples, her kings, a hundred cubits high, whom she seated in her oasis, above the motionless wheat, their foreheads in the solitude of the heavens. Their hands have never left their knees. They refuse to speak. One must consider them profoundly and seek in the depth of oneself the echo of their mute confidences. Then their somnolence is awakened confusedly. . . . The science of Egypt, its religion, its despair, and its need for eternity—that endless murmur of ten thousand monotonous years—the whole of it is contained in the sigh which the colossus of Memnon exhales at sunrise.

THE EUPHRATES AT BABYLON

Chapter III. THE ANCIENT ORIENT

I

ERE, between the two old rivers which empty into the burning sea after crossing the solitudes, there is no longer anything more than formless hillocks, choked canals, and a few poor villages. The sand has covered up everything. Doubtless it is not much deeper above the Chaldean palaces which have disappeared than around the temples of the Nile which are still visible at its surface; and the Greeks must have exaggerated when they assigned two hundred thousand years of antiquity to Babylonian civilization. But the material of the walls was less hard and their abandonment by men more complete. And what, then, does it matter? The true cradle of the human soul is wherever we can recognize the face of our earliest aspiration.

THE ANCIENT ORIENT

And yet how mobile this face is! There it glows with the light of an undying hearth of contemplative aspirations, here we see concentrated the rigorous will to attain the visible and practical purpose and not to

CHALDEA (XXX Century B.C.?). Lion (*Louvre*).

go beyond it. The statues, which the dunes covered in the ruins of Tello, bear witness to a mind infinitely more positive, if not more sure of itself, than ever the Egyptian mind was, even at the time of the "Seated Scribe," their contemporary by a margin of a few centuries; and in the old Orient centuries count no more than years. Egypt had probably built the Pyramids by then, and had given the Sphinx's visage to a rock; the next age was to plunge her still deeper into mystery and turn her gaze inward more and more. The statues of Tello are neither gods nor symbols; they have nothing mysterious about them but their

80   ANCIENT ART

antiquity and that silence which haunts the old stones found amid the relics of life beneath the ground. Here is the image of a builder-prince, a rule across his knees. As in Egypt, it is true, these decapitated bodies are stiff; rigid planes cut them into rectangular figures, and the limbs remain at rest; but the shoulders have

CHALDEA. Archaic figures (*British Museum*).

a terrible squareness, and the hands, instead of reposing on the thighs in the abandon of thought, are joined and strongly clasped, as if to indicate the articulation of the bones, the moving relief of the muscles, the folds and the rough grain of the skin. Two heads found near them have the same energy. One would think they were natural rocks that had been rolled by the waters, such is their compactness, their coherence, their sustained roundness.

In facial feature primitive Mesopotamia was, however, the sister of the plain of the Nile. The Tigris and the Euphrates, whose alluvial deposits nourish Mesopotamia, penetrate the country through hundreds of canals which cross one another around the cultivated fields. Covered with palm trees and date trees,

CHALDEA (XXX Century B.C.?). Palace of Tello, head, stone (*Louvre*).

with fields of wheat and barley, always at its harvest time, always at its seed time, Mesopotamia was the Eden of the Biblical legends, the granary of western Asia, to which its caravans and its rivers brought fruits and bread. By way of the Persian Gulf it launched its fleets on the sea. But renewing its strength from the tribes which descended from the high plateaus, communicating by its rivers connected with the oceans of the south, with Armenia and with Syria which bounds the European Sea, surrounded by more advanced and more accessible peoples, it remained less shut in than Egypt, and did not, like the latter, consume itself at its own flame. To the east it made fecund the Medo-Persian Empires, and through them penetrated into India and even into China. To the north it extended itself through Assyria until the dawn of the modern civilizations. To the west it awakened Phœnicia, which opened the route from Mesopotamia to the valley of the Nile and to the world of the archipelago.

Finally, the Chaldean theocracy probably adhered more closely to primitive instincts than the priestly caste did that governed the people of the Nile. It was in Chaldea that astronomy was born, to which her engineers of hydraulics and her architects added the unerring instruments of geometry and mechanics. It was during her brilliant nights, when the earth prolongs its glow, which is due to the cloudless sky and the flatness of the land, that the shepherds of the earliest times, as well as those who came later to seek the coolness of the upper terraces, had observed in the clear sky the turning of the constellations. The positivistic education of the Egyptians aimed at more material needs and, because of this, left untouched the source of the great moral intuitions to which the people turned for a consolation, and which the Chaldean people, less harshly governed, interpreted in terms of navigation and trade, while the king-priests

CHALDEA (xxx Century B.C.?). Statue of Goudea (*Louvre*).

of Babylon interpreted it in the higher serenity which comes with the contemplation of the movements of the heavenly bodies.

Before the time of those powerful statues, which seem to foretell the end of this people's evolution and which are certainly the final flower of a culture centuries old, Chaldean art is almost an entire mystery. Its baked clay, less hard than the granite of the valley of the Nile or the marble of Pentelicus, has turned to dust; nothing is left but some sunken foundations. Only stone, which is scarce in Mesopotamia, can resist under the tide of earth that gnaws and corrodes like water and ends by reclaiming everything. From Assyro-Chaldean positivism to Egyptian idealism we find the distance which separates the consistency of baked clay from that of granite. Between the soil of the country and the intelligence of men, there

ASSYRIA (IX Century B.C.). Genius with the head of an eagle, bas-relief (*Louvre*).

THE ANCIENT ORIENT

have always been such close analogies which we find are logical and necessary as soon as we understand that the mind invents nothing—discovers everything. We see, therefore, that a material which endures ought to give it the idea of permanence, and that a material

ASSYRIA (VIII Century B.C.). Decoration of a door of Nimrod, bas-relief (*Louvre*).

which crumbles should give it the idea of fragility and of the practical utilization of the instruments it can furnish. Thus, also, a sky whose mathematical revolutions have been scrutinized gives the idea of consecrating the precise means which it offers for mapping it out.

And so has disappeared the very skeleton of those monstrous cities which sheltered the most active peoples of the ancient world, and the most practical, in the modern sense of the word. Where Babylon rose there is nothing but palm groves on some vestiges of city walls, around which the sand heaps up. None the less, on the two banks of the Euphrates, Babylon encircled its multitudes in a belt of walls twenty-five leagues in length, ninety feet in thickness, bristling with two hundred and fifty towers and studded with gates of bronze. Built of bricks and bitumen, with its city walls, palaces, temples, houses, street pavements, the banks of its canals, its reservoirs, the bridges and quays of the river—uniform, dull, and reddish in color, here and there touched with enamel, the city of Semiramis lifted toward the heavens its monotonous buildings, almost solid blocks with gardens on their terraces, thus resembling the Iranian foothills, which are bare as far up as the cool plateaus, where forests and flowers grow. Above these artificial woods were towers, made up of stages built one upon the other. The plains call for gigantic constructions from which they can be surveyed from afar and commanded, and which shall be infinite like themselves. The tower of Babel was never to be finished and, as if to explore the ocean of the stars from nearer by, the temple of Baal rose to a height of two hundred meters.

The tower of Babel is now a formless hill which the desert is absorbing little by little. Apart from the seals of hard stone which continued to be produced during the whole civilization of Nineveh, there is perhaps no longer much that is solid under the sand, and it is possible that Chaldea has nothing more to

THE ANCIENT ORIENT

reveal to us. The sand still gives up, at times, one of those cuneiform inscriptions which are the most ancient writing known, and by which the Chaldeans

ASSYRIA (VIII Century B.C.). King fighting, bas-relief (*British Museum*).

wrote their legal documents, their acts of purchase and of sale, the great events of their history, the recital of the deluge—history and legend intermingled. The few bas-reliefs of Tello must have been an exception in the industry of the time. The desert is too bare to inspire in man the desire for multiple forms and luxuriant decoration. It needs, rather, the outer life of the Assyrians with their wars and hunts, to bring about a more prolonged contact with living forms. But it brings about nothing which is not strongly indicated in the bas-relief of Tello, where vultures carry off in their claws and tear with their beaks strips of human bodies, and in the dense black statues with prominent muscles.

II

The art of northern Mesopotamia inherits from Babylonian art just as Ninevite civilization did from Chaldean society. The language which its artists speak is about the same, for the soil, the sky, and the men are not very different. Only, with the transformation of the social order and the conditions of life, Chaldean positivism has become brutality. The priest-savant has given place to the military chief, who has usurped to his profit and that of his class the temporary command which his companions in hunting and in battle intrusted to him. The king, in Assyria, is no longer, as in Egypt, the figurehead and instrument of the priest; he is the Sar, the temporal and spiritual chief, obeyed under pain of death. The Assyrian astronomer knows Chaldean science, to be sure, but his role is limited to compelling the heavenly bodies to voice the desires and interests of his master. Chaldean star worship, an essentially naturalistic and positivistic religion, has been transformed with the social state. The symbols have been personified just as political power was; the sun, the planets, and fire are now real beings—terrible devourers of men, and the Sar is their armed hand.

This Sar is saturated with hereditary vices, deformed, before he comes to reign, by an autocracy centuries old. He is developed in a frightful solitude by a

Assyria (VIII Century B.C.). Officer, bas-relief (*Louvre*).

world of women, of eunuchs, of slaves, officers, and ministers. Luxury and the weight of material life have crushed his heart. He is a sadistic beast. He is enervated with ennui, with indulgence and music,

Assyria (viii Century B.C.). The fisherman, bas-relief
(*British Museum*).

with the smells of slaughter and of flowers. Men are burned or boiled for his gratification; he is shown living flesh which is being torn by the whip or cut by iron, and in which poison is producing lockjaw. His least impulse is expressed by an order to kill. On the bas-reliefs of Khorsabad and Koujoundjik, we may see him methodically putting out the eyes of chained prisoners; we may see his soldiers bowling with decapitated heads. Sennacherib, Sargon, or Assurbanipal orders his scribes to write on brick:

"My war chariots crush men and beasts and the bodies of my enemies. The monuments which I erect are made of human corpses from which I have cut the heads and the limbs. I cut off the hands of all those whom I capture alive."

Suffering exists in proportion to sensibility. It is

Assyria (VIII Century B.C.). Lioness resting, bas-relief (*British Museum*).

possible that the Assyrian people did not feel the horror of living, since they never felt its real joy as did the Egyptian crowds, which confided to the granite of the tombs the sweetness and poetry of their soul. Killing is an intoxication. By dint of seeing blood flow, by dint of expecting death, one grows to love blood, and everything that one does in life smells of death. Massacre always; battles, and the military tide rising or ebbing to carry devastation round about Nineveh or to turn it back upon the surrounding peoples. Always the swarming of the nameless masses in putrefaction and misery, in the poisonous vapors of the waters and the devouring fire of the heavens.

When this people is not cutting throats or burning buildings, when it is not decimated by famine and butchery, it has only one function—to build and decorate palaces whose vertical walls shall be thick enough to protect the Sar, his wives, his guards, and his slaves—twenty or thirty thousand persons—against the sun, invasion, or perhaps revolt. Around the great central courts are the apartments covered with terraces or with domes, with cupolas, images of the absolute vault of the deserts, which the Oriental soul will rediscover when Islam shall have reawakened it. Higher than these, observatories which are at the same time temples, the *zigurats*, the pyramidal towers whose stages painted with red, white, blue, brown, black, silver, and gold, shine afar through the veils of dust which the winds whirl in spirals. Especially at the approach of evening, the warring hordes and the nomadic pillagers, who see the somber confines of the desert streaked with this motionless lightning, must recoil in fear. It is the dwelling of the god, and resembles those steps of the plateau of Iran leading to the roof of the world, which are striped with violent colors by subterranean fire and by the blaze of the sun.

The gates are guarded by terrific brutes, bulls and lions with human heads, marching with a heavy step. On the whole length of the interminable walls they herald the drama which unrolls within—the mytho-

THE ANCIENT ORIENT

logical and living hell, the slaughter of men in war, the men falling from the tops of towers into the shower of stones and spears, kings choking lions, the bloody epic whose cruelty is increased by its mechanical expression. These stiff legs in profile, those torsos

Assyrian Art (viii Century B.C.). Basket, model in stone (*British Museum*).

seen in profile or front view, these arms articulated like pincers—all are resisting, some killing, some dying. And if this life thus formed never attains that silent rhythm which, in Egypt, communicates to it a character of such high spirituality, it gives the ferocious bas-reliefs of the palaces of Nineveh a force so rigorous as to seem to pursue its demonstration by its own impetus.

It is by this burst of life, arrested in a few attitudes —conventional but passionately alive—that all archaisms correspond one with another. Certain writers have tried, by a too easy process of reasoning, to associate the ancient forms of art with the attempts of children. The Egyptians and the Assyrians are supposed to have traced mere sketches of a superior figure, which was to be realized by the Greeks. As in the images made by children, it is true, the eye is seen in front view and very wide, illuminating a face in profile. It is true that the Theban or Ninevite artist satisfied the need for continuity, which the child also shares with all beings and which is the very condition of his logical development; he did so in following— untiringly and willingly—the uninterrupted line of the contours, the definition of the eye by the edge of the lids, and the profile of the face, whose plane flees and floats as soon as it is presented in front view. But it is only in decorative bas-relief or in painting— the language of convention—that Egypt and Assyria reveal this inadequacy of technique—which, however, takes away nothing from the force of the sentiment and leaves intact the incomparable conception of mass and of evocative line. Assyrian art and Egyptian art represent a synthetic effort whose profundity and whose power of intuition are such that it is puerile to think childhood capable of anything similar. And when the Egyptian turns to his true means of expression—sculpture—he reveals in it a science which will never again contain so much ardor and mystery, even if the social and moral preoccupations of other peoples animate it with a different life, indeed a freer and more comprehensive life. The art of the old peoples

THE ANCIENT ORIENT

develops itself within itself; it accepts the fixed limits of the great metaphysical systems and thus is prevented from expressing the multiple and infinitely complex relationships between the being in movement and the world in movement. Only political and

ASSYRIA (VIII Century B.C.) The lion hunt, bas-relief (*British Museum*).

religious liberty will break the archaic mold, to reveal to man, who is already defined in his structure, his place in the universe.

Assyrian society was particularly far removed from such preoccupations. It was interested only in adventures of war or of hunting in which the Sar was the hero. The walls of his palace declare his glory and his strength. No desire to better life, no moving tenderness. When they did not celebrate a killing they showed a line of soldiers on the march to a killing.

When the Assyrians left their burning soil to go down to the sea they saw nothing but the effort of the rowers, they leaned over the waves only to see fish seized by crabs. There was nothing like this in Egypt, which again and again took refuge in that concentration of mind which gives a quality of inner life and a mystery to its art. There is nothing like this even in Chaldea, where we find feminine bodies outlined in a furtive caress. Amid the incessant wars, the invasions, ruins, and griefs, the artist had not the time to look within him. He served his master, and without mental reservations. He followed him in his military expeditions against Chaldea, against Egypt, against the Hittites, and the tribes of the high plateaus. In his train he hunts the onager in the plains, or goes with him to seek the lion in the caverns of the Zagros Mountains. He leads a violent life, full of movement, and not at all contemplative. He recounts it with brutality.

Assyrian art is of a terrible simplicity. Although an almost flat silhouette, one that is barely shadowed by undulations, alone marks out the form—that form is bursting with life, movement, force, savage character. One might say that the sculptor ran a knife over the course of the nerves which carry the murderous energy to the back, the limbs, and the jaws. The bones and muscles stretch the skin to the breaking point. Hands clutch paws, close upon necks, and draw the bowstring; teeth tear, claws rend; the blood spouts thick and black. Only the human face is without movement. Never does one see its surface light up with the dull

Assyria (viii Century B.C.). Wild beasts wounded and dead, bas-relief (*British Museum*).

glow of the Egyptian faces. It is altogether exterior, always the same—hard, closed, very monotonous, but very much characterized by its immense eyes, its arched nose, its thick mouth, its dead and cruel ensemble. It is meet that the king, whose head retains its tiara and its oiled, perfumed, and curled hair and beard, should be calm as he strangles or cuts the throat of the monster, drunk with fury. It is meet that the details of his costume, as well as those of his hairdressing, should be minutely described. The poor artist has to concern himself with pitiful things. He flatters his master, ornaments his garments, and cares for his weapons and war equipment; he makes his hair glossy; he represents him as being impassible and strong in combat, larger than those who accompany him, dominating without effort the furious beast which he kills. The terrible character of the breasts, the legs, the arms in action, the wild animals rushing to the attack with muscles tense, bones cracking, or jaws grinding, is too often masked by the artist.

What matter? At that time when a man could not free himself he had to assume his share of the servitude. The Ninevite artist comprehended—that is, the one really accessible liberty. He was infinitely stronger than those whose horrible power he had the weakness to adore. The too elegant, the too courageous Sars with their royal ornaments and their trappings, bore us, and that is the revenge of the sculptor. What he loved seizes us—overpowers us. Ask him how he saw the animals: lean horses with thin legs, nervous, drawn heads, with throbbing nostrils; ask

THE ANCIENT ORIENT

him to show you the growling dogs as they pull at their chains, or the bristling lions, or the great birds run through by arrows and falling among the trees. There he is incomparable, superior to all before and after him, Egyptians, Ægeans, Greeks, Hindoos, Chinese, Japanese, the Gothic image makers, and the

ASSYRIA (VIII Century B.C.). The trophies of the hunt, bas-relief (*British Museum*).

men of the Renaissance in France or in Italy. Under the palm trees with their rough-skinned fruits he has surprised the beast at rest, its muzzle resting on its paws as it digests the blood it has drunk. He has seen the beast in combat, tearing flesh, opening bellies, mad with hunger and rage. The forces of instinct circulate with blind violence in these contracted muscles, these beasts falling heavily on the prey, these bodies raised upright, with limbs apart and open claws, in these wrinkling muzzles, these irresistible springs, and these death struggles as ferocious as leaps or victories. Never will uncompromising description go farther. Here a lion vomits blood because his lungs are run through by a spear. There a lioness in fury, her teeth and claws out, drags toward the hunter her body paralyzed by the arrows that have pierced the marrow of her spine. They are still terrible when dead, lying on their backs, with their great paws falling idly. It is the poem of strength, of murder, and of hunger.

Even when he puts aside for a day his subjects of battle or the chase, his orgies of murder in the horrible chorus of death clamors and roars, the Assyrian sculptor continues his poem. Almost as well as the sphinxes of the sacred alleys of Egypt, the violent monsters who guard the gates give that impression of animal unity which makes the strangest creations of our imagination re-enter the order of nature. But the statue maker of Nineveh is not content with fixing an eagle's head on the shoulders of a man, a man's head on the neck of a bull. The bull, the lion, the eagle, and the man are merged; we get the body or claws of a lion, the hoofs or breast of a bull, the wings or claws of an eagle, the hard head of a man, with his long hair, beard, and high tiara. Man and lion, eagle and bull, the being has always the potentiality of life; in its brutal and tense harmony it fulfills its symbolic function, and its violent synthesis of the natural forms represents to our eyes the power of the armed animal. As in Egypt, the head of the monster is generally human—an obscure and magnificent homage rendered by the man of violence to the law which man bears essentially within him, the law which says that blind force is to be overcome by the force of the mind.

III

On the horizon of the ancient world this disciplined force was rising slowly. The peoples who received from Assyria the heritage of our conquests and who already had taken over from Iranian husbandry its cult of bread and the plow, the worship of fire, the central force of civilized life, the first philosophic notions of good and evil, which Ormuzd and Ahriman personified—the people of the mountains of the East were entering history with an ideal less harsh. Masters of the high plateaus, the Medes, after long struggles, had overturned the empire of the rivers, to spread over Asia Minor. Then Cyrus had given the hegemony to the Persians, and soon all western Asia, from the Persian Gulf to the Euxine Sea, Syria, Egypt, Cyrenaica, Cyprus, and the banks of the Indus obeyed his successors. Only the breasts of the Greeks could stop the wave at Marathon. But this incessant binding together of men and ideas had done its work. If the armies of the King of Kings remained subject to the frightful discipline which they inherited from the Sars of Assyria, political Persia at least left to the countries it had just conquered the liberty to live about as they pleased. The enormous Medo-Persian

ANCIENT ART

Empire became a kind of federal monarchy whose component states, under the direction of the satraps, kept their customs and their laws. The atmosphere

PHŒNICIAN ART. Frieze (*Louvre*).

of the Oriental world became more tolerable, as was the case in the Occident when Rome had conquered it entirely. Men cultivated their fields and exchanged their merchandise and ideas in comparative peace. The attempt at a first synthesis, even, was about to be made among the peoples of the Levant.

THE ANCIENT ORIENT

That attempt would hardly produce a final result either in Egypt or in Greece. Egypt, fatigued by forty or sixty centuries of effort, was being swallowed up under the deposits of the river. Greece was too

Hispano-Phœnician Art (v Century B.C.).
Head from Elche (*Louvre*).

young and too much alive not to extract a personal ideal of victory from all the elements that the ancient world intrusted to her. As to the people of Syria, they had already failed in various attempts which they had made. The Phœnicians lived only for trade. They were forever on the sea, or on the search for unknown coasts, possessed with a fever for wandering which was fed by their mercantile nature. Mingling with the Mediterranean peoples whom they flooded with their products—textiles, vases, glassware, wrought metals, trinkets, statuettes hastily imitated from all the original nations for whom they were the agents and intermediaries—they had not the time to question their hearts. They were satisfied to serve as a means of exchange for the ideas of others and to bequeath to the world the alphabet, a positivist invention which the extent and complication of their commercial writings rendered necessary. Cyprus, the eternally servile, subjected to their influence, combined fallen Assyria with nascent Greece in heavy and doughlike forms wherein the force of the one and the intelligence of the other were reciprocally hurtful in the attempt to unite them. As to the Hittites, caught between the Egyptians and the Assyrians and pushed into northern Syria, they were never sufficiently masters of themselves to seek in the outer world any justification of their desire to cut stone into those rude bas-reliefs on which remains the moral imprint of the conqueror.

The Semites, through the gravity and the vigor of their history, might have had the ambition to pick up the instrument of human education which Assyria was letting fall—the more so since they had absorbed, by peaceful conquest, the populations of Mesopotamia, and since their race dominated from Iran to the sea. But their religion repudiated the cult of images. Their whole effort was employed in raising a single edifice, the house of a terrible and solitary god. And

THE ANCIENT ORIENT

that effort did not produce a final result. The Temple of Solomon was not worthy of that Jewish genius, so grandly synthetical, but closed and jealous, which

PERSIA. Palace of Persepolis.

wrote the poem of Genesis, and whose voice of iron has traversed the ages.

Persia alone, mistress of the hearths of Oriental civilization, could—by concentrating for a final leap the weakening energies of the peoples she had conquered—attempt a résumé of the soul of antiquity, in the course of the two hundred years which separated her appearance in the world and the Macedonian conquest. Egypt, Assyria, and Greece—she assimilated the qualities of all. For two centuries she represented the Oriental spirit declining in face of the Occidental spirit which was issuing from the shadow.

She had even the exceptional destiny not to disappear entirely from history and to show to changing Europe —now very civilized, now very barbarous—a genius sufficiently supple to welcome, in their turn, the ideas of the Hellenic world, the Latin world, the Arab world, the world of the Hindoos and of the Tartars; and yet her genius was sufficiently independent to emancipate her from their material domination.

If we refer to the testimony of her most ancient monuments, of the period when she was trying to disengage a freer and less tense spirit from the force of Assyria, we perceive quickly that the archers of her processions are not so cruel, that the beasts whose throats are cut are not so fearful, that the monsters which guard the gates or support the architraves have a less brutal look. The hieratic spirit of conquered Egypt and especially the harmonious intelligence of the Ionians of the coasts and islands who were called in by Darius give to these feasts of death a character of decoration and pageantry which masks their ferocity. The genius of Greece, which was then ripening, could not endure an original form of art subsisting at its side. And as it could not prevent Persia from speaking, it denatured her words in translating them. It is not even necessary to see the Assyrian monsters before looking at the figures of Susa in order to realize that the latter have but little life, that they are heraldic in their silhouette and rather bombastic in style. The Sassanian kings, their prisoners, and the great military scenes cut in the rock at several places in the mountain chain which

THE ANCIENT ORIENT

borders the Iranian plains and dominates the region of the rivers, have a far more grand and redoubtable appearance, despite the discernible evidence that Persia continued to borrow from the peoples with

PERSIA (VI Century B.C.). Frieze of the Archers at Susa (*Louvre*).

whom she fought—the Romans after the Greeks and Assyrians. Asia alone and Egypt have possessed the unshakable and gigantic faith that is needed to stamp the form of our sentiments and of our acts on these terrible natural walls against which the sun crushes men, or to spend three or four centuries in penetrating the bowels of the earth in order to deposit in its shade the seed of our mind.

Amid these sculptured mountains we find the ruins of the great terraced palaces to which giant staircases lead and for the building of which Ninevite architects had certainly come; and we are astonished that Greek genius, which in the same centuries was building its small and pure temples, could have made itself pliable to the point of marrying without effort its own grace and this brutal display of pomp and sensuality, before which the serenity of the Egyptian genius bowed ever as did the violence of the Assyrian genius. It was, however, Ionian Greece that gave the elegance and the upward thrust to the long columns of the porticos, as she also draped the archers and gave architectural style to the lions. It was Egypt that loaded their bases and necks with strong wreaths of plants—lotus and fat leaves that grow in the tepid water of the rivers. It was Assyria that crowned them with broad bulls affixed by the middle of the body to support the beams on which the entablature was to be placed. And the palaces of Nineveh seemed to have piled up here their chiseled furniture with its incrustation of gold, silver, and copper, their cloths heavy with precious stones and those thick deep carpets, changeable in color and shaded like the harvests of the earth, opulent and vague like the Oriental soul— the carpets which Persia had not ceased to manufacture. But the decoration of the royal dwellings of Persepolis and of Susa is less loaded, less barbarous, and betokens a more refined industry and a mind that is humanizing. Enameled brick, with which the Assyrians, after the Chaldeans, had protected

PERSIA (III Century B.C.). Valerian in supplication before Sapor, sculptured rock of Nakche-Roustem, after Dieulafoy in *L'Art Antique de la Perse* (Librairie des Imprimeries Réunies).

their walls against humidity, is lavished from the top to the bottom of the edifice, on the exterior, under the porticos, and in the apartments. The palace of the Achemenides is no longer the impenetrable fortress of the Sars of the north. Still imposing by its rectangular heaviness, it is lightened by its columns, which have the freshness of stalks swelling with water; it is flowered with green, blue, and yellow, brilliant as lacquer in the sunlight, and reflecting the glow of the lamps. Enamel is the glory of the Orient. It is still enamel which reflects the burning days and the nights of tawny pearl in the cupolas and the minarets of the mysterious cities sunk under the black cypresses and the roses.

When Alexander reached the threshold of these palaces, dragging behind his war chariots all the old vanquished peoples, he was like the incarnate symbol of the ancient civilizations wandering in search of their dispersed energy. His dream of universal empire was to endure a shorter time than that of Cambyses and his successors. Union is to be realized only when willed by a common faith and when it tends toward one goal. Egypt, Chaldea, and Assyria, exhausted by their gigantic production, were nearing the end of their last winter. The Jews, in their inner solitude, were marching toward a horizon that no one perceived. Rome was too young to impose on the Orient, now grown old, that artificial harmony which, three centuries later, gave it the illusion of a halt in its lethargic death struggle. Greece, in her skepticism, smiled at her own image. Meanwhile, the

Macedonian was pretending to the position of armed apostle of her thought, and the whole ancient world was under her moral ascendancy. Despite all, in that immense floating mass of civilizing energies which hesitated about their departure for a more distant Occident, it was still Greece that represented, in the face of the confused reawakening of brutal and mystical powers, the young ideal of reason and liberty.

Persia (Sassanide). Silver cup (*Bibliotheque Nationale*).

MYCENÆ.

Chapter IV. THE SOURCES OF GREEK ART

I

N condition that we respect ruins, that we do not rebuild them, that, after having asked their secret, we let them be recovered by the ashes of the centuries, the bones of the dead, the rising mass of waste which once was vegetations and races, the eternal drapery of the foliage—their destiny may stir our emotion. It is through them that we touch the depths of our history, just as we are bound to the roots of life by the griefs and sufferings which have formed us. A ruin is painful to behold only for the man who is incapable of participating by his activity in the conquest of the present.

There is no more virile luxury than that of asking our past griefs how they were able to determine our present actions. There is no more virile luxury than that of demanding, from the imprints of those who prepared our present dwelling, the why of the thing

ÆGEAN PERIOD (XIX Century B.C.).
Phæstos, vase of the reapers, steatite
(*Museum of Candia*).

that we are. A statue coming all moist out of the earth, a rusted jewel, or a bit of pottery bearing the trace of painting is a witness which tells us much more about ourselves than about the bygone men who uttered this testimony. Art lives in the future. It is the fruit of the pain, desires, and hopes of the people, and the promise contained in these feelings does not reach its slow realization until later, in the new needs of the crowds; it is our emotion which tells us if the old presentiments of men did not deceive them.

If we are so troubled by the rude idols, the jewels,

THE SOURCES OF GREEK ART 115

the vases, the pieces of bas-reliefs, and the effaced paintings which we have found at Knossos in Crete, at Tirynth and Mycenæ in Argolis, it is precisely

CRETE (xv Century B.C.). The goddess with the serpents, faïence statuette (*Museum of Candia*).

because those who left them are more mysterious to us than the things themselves, and because it is comforting for us to realize, through these unknown beings, that under the variation of appearances and the renewal of symbols, emotion and intelligence never change in quality. Through the continuing action, even when obscure and without history, of the generations which have formed us, the soul of the old peoples lives in ours. But they participate in our own adventure only if their silent spirit still animates the stone faces in which we recognize our eternally young desires, or if we hear the sound of their passage over the earth in the crumbling of the temples which they raised. Egypt, and Chaldea itself, through Assyria and Persia which prolong their life till our time, cast their shadow at our steps. They will never seem to us very far away. Primitive Greece, on the contrary, which does not enter the world until centuries after them, retreats much farther back in the imagination, to the very morning of history. Twenty years ago we did not know whether the almost effaced imprints, noted here and there on the shores and islands of the Ægean Sea, had belonged to men or to fabled shadows. It was necessary to hollow out the soil, to unearth the stones, and to cease from seeing only ourselves in them, in order to catch a glimpse of the phantom humanity which, before the time of history, peopled the eastern Mediterranean. Schliemann, who took Homer at his word, excavated in the plain off Argos from Tirynth to Mycenæ. Mr. Evans entered the labyrinth of Minos in Crete where Theseus killed the Minotaur. Myth and history entangle themselves. Now the symbol sums up a hundred events of the same order; now the real event, representative of a whole series

THE SOURCES OF GREEK ART 117

of customs, ideas, and adventures, seems to us to put on the garb of a symbolic fiction.[1]

Is it the body of Agamemnon that Schliemann found, buried in gold, under the Agora of Mycenæ, and is the Hissalrik of the Dardanelles the Troy of Homer? What matter? Between Abraham and Moses, in the time when Thebes dominated Egypt, the Ægean Sea was alive. The Phœnicians had advanced from island to island, awakening to the life of exchange the tribes of fishermen who peopled the Cyclades, Samos, Lesbos, Chios, Rhodes — the rocks sprinkled broadcast in the sparkling sea from the mountains of Crete and of the Peloponnesus to the gulfs of Asia Minor. Through them the sensual and cruel spirit of the Orient and the secret spirit of the peoples of the Nile had fertilized the waves. Danaos came from Egypt, Pelops from Asia, Cadmus from Phœnicia.

CRETE (XIV Century B.C.). Jar (*National Museum of Athens*).

---
[1] Victor Bérard, *Les Phéniciens et l'Odyssée*.

From fishing, coast trade, the small business of one isle with another, from rapine and piracy, a whole little moving world of sailors, merchants, and corsairs lived their healthy life, neither a rich nor a poor one—a mean one—if we think of the vast commercial enterprises and the great explorations which the Phœnicians undertook. Their feet in the water and their faces to the wind, the men of the Ægean would carry to the traffickers from Tyre and Sidon who had just entered the port, under blue, green, and red sails, their fish and their olives in vases painted with marine plants, octopuses, seaweed, and other forms taken from the teeming, viscous life of the deep. It needed centuries, doubtless, for the tribes of a single island or a single coast to recognize a chief, to consent to follow him afar on cunning and bloody expeditions to the cities of the continent, whence they brought back jewels, golden vessels, rich stuffs, and women. And it was only then that the Achaians and the Danai of the old poems heaped up those heavy

MYCENÆ (XIII Century B.C.). Bull's head, silver (*National Museum, Athens*).

THE SOURCES OF GREEK ART

stones on the fortified promontories, the Cyclopean walls, the Pelasgic walls under the shadow of which the Atrides, crowned with gold like the barbarian kings who sallied forth from the forests of the north two thousand years later, sat at table before the meats and wines, with their friends and their soldiers.

Such origins could not but make them subtle and hard. Æschylus felt this when he came there, after eight centuries, to listen in the solitude to the echo of the death cries of the frightful family. These pirates selected sites for their lair near the sea—tragically consistent with their life of murder and the heavy orgies which followed upon their deeds of crime.

MYCENÆAN PERIOD (XIV-XIII Centuries B.C.). Vase of Palai-Kastro, clay (*Museum of Candia*).

A circle of hills—bare, devoured by fire and enlivened by no torrent, no tree, no bird cry. We find the life of these men depicted on the sides of the rudely chiseled vase of Vaphio, and on the strips of wall remaining beneath the ruins of Tirynth and of Knossos. There are bits of frescoes there as free as the flight of the sea birds; the art is of a terrible candor, but is already disintegrating. One sees women with bare breasts, rouge on their lips, black around the eyes, their flounced dresses betraying the bad taste of the barbarian; they are painted and sophisticated dolls bought in the Orient or taken by force on the expeditions of violence. Here are bulls pursued in the olive groves, bulls gallop-

MYCENÆAN PERIOD (XII Century B.C.). Vase of Vaphio, gold (*National Museum, Athens*).

ing, rearing, charging upon men or tangled in great nets. Sometimes there are reapers who laugh and sing with tremendous gayety among the sheaves of wheat which they carry, but usually we find the questionable woman, the wild beast, and the marine monster; a voluptuous and brutal life like that of every primitive man raised to a post of command by force or by chance. As guardians of the gates of their acropolis they set up stone lionesses with bronze heads, heavily erect. When they died these men were laid away in a shroud of gold leaf. . . .

It was a civilization already rotten, a Byzantium in

miniature, where dramas of the bedroom determined revolutions and massacres. It ended like the others. The Dorian descends from the north like an avalanche, rolls over Argolis and even to Crete, devastating the cities and razing the acropolises. Legendary Greece enters a thick darkness from which she would not have reappeared if the barbarians had not left, intact under the conflagration, such material testimony of her passage through history as the kings with the masks of gold. The Phœnicians desert the coast of the Peloponnesus, of Attica, and of Crete, and the native populations, dispersed like a city of bees on which a host of wasps has descended, swarm in every direction, on the shores of Asia, in Sicily, and in southern Italy. Silence reigns around continental Greece. It was to be two or three hundred years before the Phœnicians and the Achaians, driven away by the invasion, could get back the route to its gulfs.

II

The Dorians had no word to say during the Hellenic middle ages; nothing from Asia entered their land. The ancient continent was advancing step by step, by way of the islands, prudently regaining a little of the lost territory. Melos, in need of pottery, had to wait till the Ceramists of primitive Athens had manufactured at the Dipylon, those vases with the geometrical designs which were the first sign of the reawakening of civilized life in barbarous Greece. We are here witnessing a slow dramatic ascent in the shadows of the soul, under this magnificent sky, at the center of this brilliant world. In order that the spark might kindle, it was necessary that the Dorian, the Phœnician, and the ancient Ægean who has become an Ionian, repair their broken relationships. Thereupon the flame mounted quicker to light up the virgin soil with the most dazzling focus of intelligence in history.

For this focus, the Homeric poems—echoes picked up from the annihilated world by the vanquished—and the radiant Greek myths which are elaborated confusedly along the deserted shores are the heralding dawnlights seen against this black background. The cradle of the Hellenic soul mounts with them on the chariot of the sun. In the evening, the Dorian herdsman bringing home his goats from the mountain and the Ionian sailor bringing home his bark from the sea would repeat to themselves glorious fables which carried over into images men's old intuitive notions of the phenomena of nature, or translated the struggle of their ancestors against the adverse forces of the ill-organized world. The enthusiastic naturism of the human soul in its freshness gave to its young science a robe of light, of clouds, of leaves, and of waters. The whole religion, the philosophy, the austere and charming soul of the builders of the Parthenons are in this anonymous and tangled poem which rises with the murmur of a dawn as Greece reawakens to life.

The "Greek miracle" was necessary. The whole ancient world had prepared, had willed its coming. During the fruitful silence when the Dorians were

MYCENÆ (XIII Century B.C.). The Gate of the Lions.

accumulating within themselves the strength of their soil, Egypt and Assyria kept their lead. But they were discouraged and stricken by the cold of age. The torch, as it grew paler, leaned toward a new race. They were to become the initiators of the Hellenic Renaissance, as they had been the guides for the childhood of the peoples of the Archipelago.

The Dorian barbarian, after his contact with less harsh climates, had disciplined his violence, but he remained rough, all of a piece, and very primitive. His idols, the Xoana, which he cut with a hatchet from oak and olive wood scarcely two hundred and fifty years before the Parthenon, were so rude that they seem to date farther back than the engraved bone of the reindeer hunters. It is to a totally uncultivated race that the intellectual heritage of Egypt and Asia was to fall; in exchange for their high spirituality and profound sensualism they were to demand the sweep and power of Greek virility. The inhabitants of the Dorian coasts, of the islands which occupied the center of the eastern Mediterranean, saw sails in always greater number coming toward them from the depths of the sea. Their contact with neighboring civilizations multiplied every day. At the crossing of all the maritime routes of the ancient world, they were soon to feel the whole of it moving within them.

The Greeks had the privilege of inhabiting a land so inundated, steeped and saturated with light, so clearly defined by its own structure, that the eyes of man had only to open, to draw from it its law. When man enters a bay closed in by an amphitheater of

THE SOURCES OF GREEK ART

mountains between an illuminated sky and water that rolls rays of light, as if a spring of flame welled up under its waves, he is at the center of a slightly dark sapphire set in a circle of gold. The masses and the lines organize themselves so simply, cutting such clear profiles on the limpidity of space that their essential relations spontaneously impress themselves on the mind. There is not a country in the world which addresses itself to the intelligence with more insistence, force, and precision than this one. All the typical aspects of the universe offer themselves, with the earth—everywhere penetrated by the sea, with the horizon of the sea, the bony islands, the straits, golden and mauve between two liquid masses glittering even in the heart of the night, the promontories so calm and so bare that they seem natural pedestals for our grateful soul, the rocks repeating from morning to evening all the changes of space and the sun, with the dark forests on the mountains, with the pale forests in the valleys, with the

IONIAN ART. (End of the VII Century B.C.). Artemis of Delos (*National Museum, Athens*).

hills everywhere surrounding the dry plains, and—bordered by pink laurel—the streams, whose whole course one can embrace at a glance.

Except in the north, one finds tormented lines of hills, savage ravines, sinister grottos from which subterranean vapors issue with a rumbling sound, black forests of pine and oak; except in the harsh countries of the primitive legends where man recounts his effort to overcome hostile nature, there are few, if any, terrifying appearances; the soil is hospitable, the usual climate is mild, though fairly severe in winter. Life in this land keeps close to its earth, is active without excess, and simple. Neither misery nor wealth nor poverty. Houses are of wood, clothing of skins, and there is the cold water of the torrents to wash off the dust and blood of the stadium. There is not much meat, that of the goat which grazes among the fissures of the rocks, perhaps, but there is a little wine mixed with resin and honey and kept in skins; there are milk, bread, the fruits of the dry countries, the orange, the fig, and the olive. There is nothing on the horizon or in social life which could give birth to or develop mystic tendencies. A nature religion exists, a very rough one—in the beliefs of the people, perhaps even rather coarse, but welling up from springs so pure and so poetized by the singers that when the philosophers think to oppose it they do no more than extract from it the rational conception of the world barely hidden in its symbols. Doubtless man fears the gods. But since the gods resemble him, they do not turn his life from the normal and natural relation-

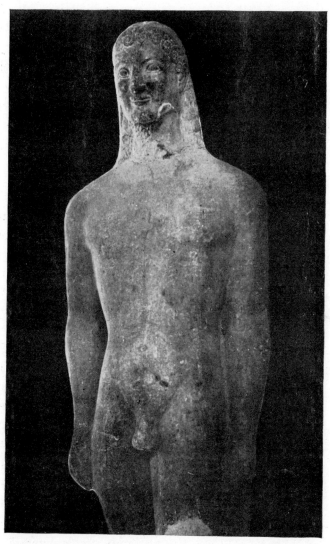

DORIAN ART (beginning of the VI Century). Athlete, known as the Apollo of Thera (*National Museum, Athens*).

ships which bind it with that of other men. The priest has but little influence. Greece is perhaps the only one of the old countries where the priest did not live outside the pale of popular life in order to represent to the people the great mysteries as a world apart. Hence the rapidity of this people's evolution and the freedom of its investigations.

III

Greece troubles herself but little, and then only at the very beginning of her art, with the enemy powers which hamper our first steps. Although man already places himself under the protection of the intelligent forces, he has not forgotten the struggles which his ancestor was forced to maintain against the brutal forces of a universe which repulsed him. This memory is inscribed in the sculptures which, on the pediment of the Parthenon of Pisistratus, showed Zeus struggling against Typhon, or Herakles throwing Echidna to earth. A barbarous work, violently painted with blues, greens, and reds, a memory of avalanches, of terrifying caverns, of the storms of the north, it was a nightmare of savages still ill taught by Asia and Egypt, but becoming curious and already

DORIAN ART (VI Century). Athlete, bronze statuette (*private collection*).

Ionian Art (580 B.C.). Hera of Samos (*Louvre*).

eager to comprehend. The hell of the pagans will last but a short time.

The temple where these idols reign, these bulls, these twisted serpents, these astonished visages with green beards, is, moreover, in its principle, what it will be in the greatest periods. Architecture is the collective, necessary art which appears first and dies first. The primordial desire of man, after food, is shelter, and it is in order to erect that shelter that, for the first time, he appeals to his faculty of discovering in natural constructions a certain logic whence, little by little, the law will issue forth and permit him to organize his life according to the plan of the universe. The forest and the cliffs are the powerful educators in the geometrical abstraction from which man is to draw the means of building houses which are to have a chance of resisting the assault of rain and storms. At Corinth there already rises a temple with heavy and very broad columns, coming straight up from the ground as they mount in a block to the entablature. Several of them still stand. They are terrible to see, black, gnawed like old trees, as hard as the mind of the Peloponnesian countries. The Doric order came from those peasant houses which one still sees in the countryside of Asia Minor, trees set in the ground in four lines making a rectangle, supporting other trees on which the roof was to be placed. The form of the pediment comes from the slope of this roof, which is designed to carry off the rain. The Greek temple, even when it realizes the most lucid and the most consciously willed intellectual

THE SOURCES OF GREEK ART

combinations, sends its roots into the world of matter, of which it is the formulated law.

On the sculptures of these temples the mind of Asia

IONIAN ART (VI Century). Hunters, carved bronze plaque (*Louvre*).

has left its trace. They are continued until the great century, but so assimilated in the nascent Hellenic genius that on seeing them one cannot think of direct imitation, but rather of those uncertain and fleeting resemblances which hover on the face of children. The archaic Dorian Apollos, those smiling and terrible statues through which force mounts like a flood, make one think, it is true, of the Egyptian forms, because of the leg which steps forward and the arms glued to the stiff torso. But on this hieratism the theocratic spirit exercises no action. Dorian art is all of a piece, far less subtle, far less refined, far less conscious than that of the sculptors of Thebes. The passages between the very brusque sculptural planes are scarcely indicated. What dominates is the need to express the life of the muscles.

It is because these Apollos are athletes. The great cult of gymnastics is born, that necessary institution which is to permit Greece to develop the strength of arms and of legs, while parallel with it there develops suppleness of the mind in its constant search for the universal equilibrium. Already, from all the regions of the Greek world, from the islands, from the distant colonies, from Italy and from Asia, the young men come to Olympia and Delphi to contest the crown of olive leaves. In running, in wrestling, and in throw-

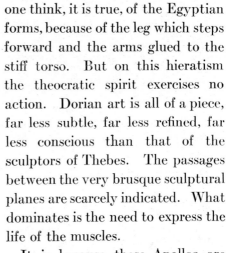

IONIAN ART (VI Century).
Athena, bronze statuette
(*National Museum, Athens*).

DORIAN ART (VI Century). Head and neck of a horse
(*Museum of Delphi*).

ing the discus they are nude. The artists, who hasten to these national meeting places, like everyone else who calls himself a Hellene, have before their eyes the spectacle of the movements of the human frame and of the complex play of the muscles rolling under the brown skin, which shows them as if they were bare themselves, and which is hardened by scars. Greek sculpture is born in the stadium. It was to take a century to climb the steps of the stadium and to install itself in the pediments of the final Parthenons, where it was to become the educator of the poets and, after them, of the philosophers. They were to feast their mind on the spectacle of the increasingly subtle relationships which sculpture established in the world of forms in action. There was never a more glorious or more striking example of the unity of our activity: athleticism, by the intermediary of sculpture, is the father of philosophy, at least, of Platonian philosophy, whose first concern was to turn against sculpture and athleticism in order to kill them.

Through the Dorian Apollo Greece passes from primitive art to archaism, properly so-called. The artist considers the form with more attention, painstakingly disengages the meaning of it, and transports that meaning to his work in so uncompromising a manner that he imposes on it the appearance of an edifice, whose architectonic quality seems destined to know no change. The Peloponnesus becomes the great training school of the archaic marble workers; Cleoethas, Aristocles, Kanakhos, and Hagelaidas open workshops at Argos, Sicyon, and Sparta; the citadel

ENDOIOS (middle of the VI Century B.C.). The Moscophorus (*Museum of the Acropolis*).

of the Dorian ideal becomes, before Athens, the focus of Greek thought. But Hellenism in its entirety is not to find its nourishment there. Sparta is far from the routes of the Old World, imprisoned in a solitary valley where mountain torrents flow; it is a fertile but a jealous country, separated from the great horizons by the hard ridges of the Taygetes, which are covered with snow even in summer. The people which dwells there is as closed as the valley itself, and it is these isolated surroundings which are for so long a time to keep up its voluntary egoism. Athens, on the contrary, is at the center of the eastern Mediterranean, and near the sea. It is the meeting point of the positive and disciplined Dorian element, which mounts from the south toward Corinth, Ægina, and Attica in its search for lands to dominate, and of the Ionian element which brings to the city, through the sieve of the islands, the artist spirit of Asia, made supple and subtle by the habits of trade, diplomacy, and smuggling. The glory of Sparta, in reality, is that of having offered to Athens a virgin soil to fertilize and also, by harassing her without mercy, to have kept her in condition, to have compelled her for a long time to cultivate her energy. Athens, tempered by these struggles, was not slow in showing her superiority. When the soldiers of Darius followed the traders of Asia to the European coast, it is she who was at the head of the Greeks, while Sparta, inclosed in the blind cult of her personal interest, took her place only after the combat.

Where are we to find the first step of Ionian art in

its march toward Attica—the uncertain dawn of the great Oriental sensualism rendered healthy by the sea and sharpened by commerce, which will flood the Dorian soul with humanity? The Hera of Samos is, perhaps, even stiffer than the Peloponnesian athletes, as it is nearer to Saite Egypt, which is unfolding at this moment and investing hieratic form with a humanity of its own. A tight sheath of cloth imprisons the legs, which are close together, but under the figure's light veil, with its lines like those on water, the shoulders, the arms, the breast, and the hollowed back have profiles of a moving grace, and planes which meet one another and interpenetrate with the delicacy of a confession. It is this spirit of abounding tenderness which is soon to take root on the Greek continent. From the end of the sixth century Dorian art and Ionian art were neighbors everywhere without having yet recognized each other fully. At Delphi, at the threshold of the Treasury of the Cnidians, Asiatic Greece saluted with a mysterious smile the rude statue maker of the Peloponnesus who had set up the women, the lions, and the formidable horses in the pediment of the Sanctuary of Apollo. The caryatids which supported the Asiatic architrave were strange, secret women; they had a winged grace, like that of an animal and of a dance; they seemed to guard the gate of temptation, which led to a warmth within, like that of the sun, and to untasted intoxications. The Dorian spirit and the Ionian spirit—the young countryman bursting with vigor and the woman bedecked, caressing, questionable—met and loved.

Attic art, which in its adult age was to be the great classic sculpture, austere and living, was to be born of their union.

IV

Marble had been skillfully treated in Athens for more than a hundred years, and the Acropolis, especially at the time of Pisistratus, had been covered with monuments and statues. But Endoios, the great Athenian master of the sixth century, still remained subject to Ionian traditions. It was only on the eve of the Median wars that the Hellenic synthesis, before manifesting itself by the collective action of resistance to the invader, is outlined in certain minds.

Undoubtedly, a people is too complex an organism, and one whose generating elements merge too closely and are too numerous to permit us to determine the degree of influence of each one of these elements in all the acts which express the people. It is like a river made up of a hundred streams, of a thousand torrents or brooks which bring to it, mixed together, the snow swept down by avalanches, the mud of clay countries, sand and flint, and the coolness and aroma of the forests it has crossed. It is the river, a broad living unity, rolling the same waters with the same sound. The men working at a particular period supply all the intermediary degrees which the future needs in order to pass from one group of men to another without effort and without finding in them differences of aspiration, though they themselves had imagined that they differed profoundly. And the men of this time

IONIAN ART (end of VI Century B.C.). Caryatid of the Treasury of the Cnidians, detail (*Museum of Delphi*).

are united to those who precede them and to those who follow them by necessary relationships wherein the mysterious continuity of our activity is manifested. It is not possible to fix the moment or to designate the work in which the Hellenic soul, as we call it to-day, tried to define itself for the first time. We can only turn our eyes to those works which possess the first quiver of life, over which there seems to pass the first breath of liberty and spiritual joy, in order that we may surprise in them the awakening of a new humanity to the beauty of living.

The young women found near the Erechtheion, twenty years ago, amid the rubbish of the foundations of the Parthenon, where the Greek workmen had put them after the sacking and burning of the Acropolis by the soldiers of Xerxes, were, perhaps, the first who had the smile of intoxication which announces the awakening. Undoubtedly the perfume of the islands was predominant with them. They think above all of pleasing; they are feminine; an invincible amorous force shines from them and accompanies them with a murmur of desire. But on seeing the surety of their planes and their definite and powerful equilibrium, we cannot doubt that the Dorian artisan, who was then working at Ægina, Corinth, and even Athens, had had repeated contacts with the Ionian immigrant whom the Persian conquest had driven back to the Occident.

Brought from the Orient by the adventurers of the sea—the men who told such lying, intoxicating, and savage tales—these women take good care not to

THE SOURCES OF GREEK ART

shock the hard, austere world which they have come to visit. They remain motionless, holding up their robes with one hand. Their red hair, which hangs on their backs and whose tresses fall on each side of their necks to rest on their breasts, is plaited and curled; it is dyed, doubtless, and streams with jewels. Sometimes their foreheads are diademed, their wrists encircled with bracelets, their ears loaded with rings. From head to foot they are painted, with blue, red, ochre, and yellow, and their eyes of enamel glow in their smiling faces. These creatures so barbarously illuminated, dazzling and bizarre as the birds of the tropics, have the strong savor of the painted and adorned women of the Orient; they are somewhat vulgar, perhaps, but fascinating none the less, like things from afar off, like fairy-tale beings, childish animals, pampered slaves. They are beautiful. We love them with a tenderness which cannot exhaust itself. The whole after-world has issued from their firm, slender flanks.

IONIAN ART (end of the VI Century B.C.). Orante (*Museum of the Acropolis*).

They have overturned the curious notions that were anchored in us by academic idealism. For three hundred years it regarded immaculate marble as a sentimental emblem of serenity—one which never existed, save in the minds of certain philosophers, at the hour when Greece was approaching her decline. And white marble also stood for a perfection which, it is to be hoped, we shall not attain—discontent, curiosity, and effort being the very condition of life. Until the complete unfolding of her art in any case, and probably until her fall, Greece painted her gods and her temples. Variegated with blues and reds, alive like men and women, the gods became animated at break of day, took part in the surprises and joys of the light, and moved in the depth of the gathering shadow. They belonged to the crowd that swarmed at the foot of the Acropolis, the busy, noisy, familiar crowd of a port leading to the Orient; they came out of the dirty alleys where stray dogs fought for scraps of offal. We see them pass before the shop windows where the port spreads out its quarters of mutton and lamb, its fruits, its heaps of spice, its dyed stuffs, and its glassware; they are in the colorful squares so full of cries and calls—of the odors of garlic, rotting food, and aromatic herbs. We see the naked children, the questionable traders, the sailors hardened by the wind, the women with the painted eyes, dressed in their garish clothing. The temples and the monuments covered with ochre, with vermilion, green, azure, and gold, are made up of the tones of the sky, of the space over the sea—greenish or flushed with purple, they have the colors of the sea, violet or blue, of the earth, of its dress of thin crops and dry foliage, with the milky olive trees and the black cypresses as they marry their forms to the ever-present forms, of the sinuous bays and the hills. What is the role of the statue maker? It is to balance, in the lucidity and the firmness of his intelligence, all these scattered elements, so that on their apparent chaos he may impose clear relationships and harmonious directions.

The Apollonian myth kept watch in the consciousness—obscure as yet, but solid and swelling with primitive faith—of the Athenian marble cutters. The strange women who had taken possession of the Athenian fortress could not have unnerved for more than an hour the city's resistance to the Asiatic hordes which they had preceded by only a short time. Already the element of orgy and sentimental excess represented by their polychromy had been held in check at every point by clear-cut planes and precise contours, thereby sustaining its alluring, smiling action. These planes and contours mark the Athenian's extraordinary urge toward domination of the sensual impulse by the virile health of his nascent reason. The miraculous and fatigued soul of Asia recovers its strength and its faith upon contact with this fierce energy, which it enlightens with intelligence in an unexpected exchange. We have reached the mysterious hour when the flower will unfold to the light the tremble of its petals, which till now had been pressed together in their green sheath. These idols represent, perhaps, man's finest effort to discover in his consciousness the approbation of his instinct. There is in them a tension of soul which moves us, an energy devoted wholly to searching out our agreement of an hour with a world whose secret harmony we feel to live within us. Ingenuous as youth, perverse as desire, they are as firm and as free as the will.

With them Greek archaism possessed itself completely of that architectural conception of form which may be very dangerous because it carries with it the risk of never escaping from it, as in the case of the Egyptians. It is admirable. It is necessary. It is a more elevated form in the eyes of some than the balanced expression of our earthly destiny which the fifth century was to realize among the Greeks. To adhere to it, however, is to pause over appearances of the absolute, beyond which intuition can advance no farther, and to forbid the intelligence to search out, in its relationships with the surrounding world, its general conception of humanity. It is to be afraid of approaching the mystery which we know to be impenetrable and which forever retreats, in the measure that we advance. To reproach Greek art with having been human is to reproach man for existing. And it is to forget, indeed, that the art of the fifth century, even when it broke the frames of archaic form to let the palpitation and the atmosphere of life enter them by torrents, retained all the principles which make the strength and the austerity of that form.

The Egyptian statue maker and the Greek statue maker of the earlier centuries, preoccupied solely with

IONIAN ART (end of the VI Century B.C.). Orante
(*Museum of the Acropolis*).

establishing the architecture of their ensembles before they penetrated to the dense world of gestures and feelings, discovered the law of profiles and by so doing founded the science of sculpture. But the element which animates the block, which gives life to the form, is lacking, or, at least, it takes on a metaphysical meaning which separates it a little more each day from the human significance of our activity and leads it fatally to the desert of pure abstraction which is closed on every side. Egyptian sculpture, arrested for all time in its movement, unable to extend its research, set itself the task of rendering subtle the *passage*, the wave without beginning or end which binds one plane to another; it was absorbed in this problem to the extent of losing sight of the mother form which was the point of departure for the problem; and because it thus forgot, Egyptian art died without hope of resurrection. Saite sculpture made only timid attempts at independence; it recommenced the same task, it imposed on granite and bronze the docility of clay, it saw in them the undulation of water, it let light and shade glide over them like clouds over the soil. But it exhausted itself in modulating the inflections of its dream much sooner than Theban sculpture did, because Thebes, at least, made a long effort to reach the formulation of this dream, and because after this dream nothing more remains if the external world is forever banned. Antæus needed to touch the earth again. The Greek sculptor, free to explore the world of appearances at his ease, did not fail to perceive that in discovering the relationships

THE SOURCES OF GREEK ART

of the planes he was to discover the ties which bind to man and to one another all the phenomena of the senses which reveal the universe to us. The *passage*, wherein the Egyptians saw only a metaphysical exercise—however admirable, becomes, with the Greek, the instrument of sensuous and rational investigation. After him *the passage was to the sculptural plane what philosophy is to science.*

It is on this account that we love the little painted idols, the astonished and barbarous orantes of the primitive Acropolis. They are at the point of highest tension which we find in Greek thought, at the decisive moment when human genius is to choose the path it is to take. The Median wars came. Athens, at the head of the Greek cities, gave to history one of its finest spectacles. She was to temper her physical strength in sacrifice and suffering, she was to use the repose of mind, which the war was to bring her, to bequeath to the next generation immense intellectual

Ionian Art (end of the vi Century).
Samian woman
(*Museum of the Acropolis*).

reserves that rush forth in forests of marble, tragedies, and triumphal odes. Thus always, in the course of our history, the great flowering of the mind follows the great animal effort, and the men of action engender the men of thought. We are approaching the hour when human enthusiasm had its hour of most powerful exaltation. The creatures of marble, so full of energy and sweetness, who peopled the citadel, had just been finished when the Persians mutilated them; Æschylus fights at Marathon, Pindar makes the branches of the sacred tree tremble in the wind of his verse, Sophocles, as a boy, bares his body to sing the Pæan on the shore of Salamis. Such vitality uplifts the artists who are to work among the ruins of the Acropolis, that, instead of setting up anew the statues which have been thrown to earth, they find them good enough only to support the pedestal of the statues which sleep within them.

THE ACROPOLIS OF ATHENS.

Chapter V. PHIDIAS

I

THE philosophic sculpture is born of liberty and dies because of it. The slave in Assyria could describe vividly the things he was permitted to see; in Egypt, he could give a definition of form as firm as the discipline which bowed him down, as full of nuances, as moving as the faith which sustained him. The free man alone gives life to the law, lends to science the life of his emotion, and sees that in his own mind we reach the crest of that continuing wave which attaches us to things in their entirety—until the day when science kills his emotion.

The artist of to-day is afraid of words, when he does not fall a victim to them. He is right to refrain from listening to the professional philosopher and especially to refrain from following him. He is wrong to be afraid of passing for a philosopher. Also, if we have no right to forget that Phidias followed the discourses of Anaxagoras, we recognize that he might, without

ÆGINA (beginning of the v Century). Temple of Athena.

loss, have been ignorant of metaphysics. He looked upon life with simplicity, but what he could see of it developed in him so lucid a comprehension of the relationships which, for the artist, make up its unity and continuity, that minds skillful in generalizing could extract from his work the elements out of which the modern world has come. Phidias formed Socrates [1] and Plato—unknown to themselves, doubtless—when

[1] It must be recalled that Socrates worked as a sculptor.

PHIDIAS

he materialized for them, in the clearest, the most veracious, and the most human of languages, the mysterious affinities which give life to ideas.

ATTIC ART (about 475). Demeter of Eleusis
(*National Museum, Athens*).

We see the philosophic spirit as it is born at the beginning of the fifth century, still hesitating and astonished at the daylight; it appears already in the "Charioteer" and in the statues of Ægina. Sculptural science, which is not obliged to copy form, but rather to establish the planes which reveal the profound law of structure and the conditions of equilibrium of form—sculptural science already exists. The "Charioteer" is as straight as a tree trunk; one feels the framework within it, one sees how it is defined by all its contours. It is a theorem of bronze. But in the folds of its rigid robe, in its narrow bare feet planted flat on the ground, its nervous arm and open fingers, in its muscular shoulders, its broad neck, its fixed eyes, and round cranium, a slow wave circulates which—by somewhat abrupt fits and starts—tries to convey from one plane to another the integrally conceived forces of life which determined these planes. The same implacable surfaces, the same harsh passages, are in the warriors of Ægina, with something more; there is here, in the abstract, a course which leads from one figure to another across empty space, and which thus creates a continuing whole, even if still a troubled one, lacking in suppleness and partaking of the mechanical; but in it an irresistible sense of relationship awakens; the firm flower is only half open, and it demands its full expansion.

There is no break in the conditions we are studying. The plastic evolution and the moral evolution mount in a single pure wave. Antenor has already erected the Tyrannicides on the Agora—the symbolic myths unroll in the frieze of the temples, and the great national wars mingle the divinities with the soldiers, on the pediments of Ægina. The athlete is to become the man, the man is to become the god, until the moment

Triumphant charioteer (462 B.C.).
(*Museum of Delphi.*)

when the artists, having created the god, find in him the elements of a new humanity. Polycleitus and Myron have already taken from the form of the wrestler, the runner, the charioteer, and the discus thrower the idea of those harmonious proportions which shall best define the masculine body in its function of uniting strength, skill, agility, nervous grace, and moral calm. To Polycleitus, the Dorian, belong rude and gathered power, virile harmony in repose; to Myron, the Athenian, belong virile harmony in movement, the vigor in the planes of the muscles, which show in a vibrant silence when the contracted tendons press hard on the head of the bones, when the furrows at the bottom of which repose the nerves and arteries, conveyors of energy, hollow themselves out at the moment when the tendons grow taut. The one establishes the profound architecture of the human body, its strength—like that of a bare column—and its visible symmetry, which the gesture and the modeling scarcely break in order that the theorem may be established upon sensation. The other discovers the

ATTIC ART (v Century).
Dancer, bronze statuette
(*Bibliotheque Nationale*).

DORIAN ART (V Century). Athlete
(*From the cast in the Ecole des Beaux-Arts*).

theorem in the heart of sensation itself, to which the living arabesque returns as a geometrical abstraction, with the whirl of all its volumes, with the quiver of all its surfaces. By the one, man is described in his stable form, by his vertical frame, by the sheaves of the arm and leg muscles whose precise undulations mark out or mask the skeleton, by his straight belly, broad, sonorous chest, the circle of the collar bones and the shoulder blades carrying the column of the neck, the round head with its glance which continues it without a break. By the other, he is described in his action. It remains for Phidias only to penetrate the statics of Polycleitus with the dynamics of Myron in rounder, fuller masses, defined by planes more broad and more mingled with the light—and he has made the marble glow with a higher life and given a heroic meaning to that form and this action. In a few years, which fly with the swiftness of human imagination, anthropomorphism ripens.

II

And here is an admirable thing! Even by the mouth of its comic poets who had, however, been formed by the great works and fed by the myths of the past, this race needed to proclaim its faith. Read in the "Peace" the moving, religious saying of Aristophanes: "The exiling of Phidias brought on the war. Pericles, who feared the same fate and who distrusted the bad character of the Athenians, cast away peace. . . . By Apollo, I was unaware that Phidias was related to that goddess. . . . Now I know why she is so beautiful." The whole of anthropomorphic idealism is in that speech. The Greek makes his gods in the image of man, and the god is beautiful, to the extent that man is lofty in mind.

On this simple soil, by this healthy race, religious naturalism was to reach its goal of deifying the natural and moral laws as men and women. The poet came,

DORIAN ART (about 460 B.C.). Temple of Zeus at Olympia. Combat of Centaurs and Lapiths (*Museum of Olympia*).

and his symbols gave resplendent visages to these deifications. What the Greek really adored when he was matured and liberated was the accord between his mind and the law. Whatever may have been said of it, anthropomorphism is the only religion that science has left intact, for science is the law deduced from the aspects of life by man, and only by him. Our conception of the world is the only proof we can offer of its existence and of our own.

The personified laws, the gods who have become real beings for the crowd, are not tyrants, not even the creators of men—they are other men, more accomplished in their virtue, more grandiose in their disorder. They have the faults and the impulses of men, they carry the latter's wisdom and beauty to the degree where these become fateful forces. They are the human ideal opposed by human passions, the laws which it is our business—against the resistance of egoism and of the elements of nature—to deduce from the world and to obey. Herakles combats the accident, the thing that retards and opposes our progress toward order. He enters the forests to beat the lions to death, he dries up swamps, he cuts the throats of evil men and overpowers bulls. His hairy arms, his knees, and his breast bleed from his struggle with the rocks. He protects the childhood of the organizing will against the adult brutality of things. At his side, Prometheus starts out for his conquest of the lightning —that is to say, of the mind. The Greek refuses to have anything to do with the god of terrible distances who kills the soul and the flesh through the hand of the priest. He tears the fire from him. The god nails him down with pain, but he cries out in revolt until Herakles comes to cut his bonds. By dint of willing it, man creates his own liberty.

Thus from the man to the god, from the real to the ideal, from acquired adaptions to desired adaptions, the hero threads his path. The human mind, in a splendid effort, rejoins the divine law. Polytheism organizes the primitive pantheism, and, with admirable audacity, brings out the spirit of it, little thinking that this flame, which Prometheus seized for a moment, will, when it tries to escape, consume the world. The sensation of spiritual infiniteness that Egyptian art gives, and of material infiniteness that Hindoo art gives, is not to be found in the art that expresses the Hellenic soul. We find in this art an accent of balanced harmony which it alone has, and which keeps within the limits of our intelligence. But the intelligence

DORIAN ART (about 460 B.C.). Temple of Zeus at Olympia. Centaur carrying off a Lapith (*Museum of Olympia*).

cannot grasp the beginning and the end of the melody with which it is cradled. All forms and all forces are bound together in a deep solidarity; one passes into law, passes into divinity. Doubtless, in the enormous universe of which the city is the definitive image, there are antagonisms, there are action and reaction, but all partial conflicts are effaced and melted in the intellectual order which man founds. Heraclitus has just affirmed, together with the eternal flow of things, the identity of contraries and their profound agreement in universal eurhythm.

It is this, above all, that the old pediments of Olympia

MAGNA GRÆCIA (about 450 B.C.). Temple of Neptune at Pæstum.

came to teach us. Earthquakes have shaken them from their place, man has broken them and dispersed their pieces, the overflow of the Alpheus has washed away their violent polychromy. Even as they are, with terrible gaps, often without heads, without torsos, almost always without limbs, held by iron supports, they remain one, coherent and integral as when, at the foot of Kronion in Altis, they towered over the forests peopled with statues. Inflamed with passion,

PHIDIAS

drunk with wine, the centaurs drag away the virgins. Fists and elbows strike; fingers twist and loosen the grasp of other hands; knives kill, and the great bodies sink under the ax, to the sound of the hammering hoofs, of sobs, and of imprecations. The brute dies, but the fever burns in his loins and his savage embrace

DORIAN ART (about 460 B.C.). Temple of Zeus at Olympia. Servant (*Museum of Olympia*).

tightens anew. Here everything is rude action, ardor of the new faith, violence of the old myths which retold the tale of the abductions of the primitive forests where all was menace, assault, and mysterious terror. Broad, animated modeling and surfaces cut with great strokes carry out the mood of struggle, of desire, of murder and death. And withal, a sovereign calm hovers over the scene. One might call it a surging, roaring sea which none the less forms an immense and tranquil harmony—because the wave is continuous, because the same forces hollow it out, lift it up, and make it fall forever, to arise forever.

Some Dorian Æschylus sculptured this great thing at the hour when the fusion of the Apollonian soul and of Dionysian intoxication caused tragedy to well up from the breast of orgiastic music, when a prodigious equilibrium maintained the mystic agitation in the flame of the mind; and he felt within him the tremor of an instinct of harmony which did not end with the horizon seen by his eyes. In all the things he hears other things resound, distant echoes are born to swell progressively and to die away little by little—there is in nature not a single movement of which the germ and the repercussion cannot be traced in all movements which manifest nature. In the sculpture of Olympia there is an enchaining of causes and effects which has its perfect logic, but which is still intoxicated with the discovery of itself. The mind of the artist prolongs it unbroken so that he may gather up into himself its tumult and passion. One moment more and Phidias transforms it into spiritual harmonies which mark the expansion of the intelligence into the fullness of love.

III

With him modeling is no longer a science, it is not yet a trade, it is a living thought. The volumes, the movements, the surge that starts from one angle of the pediment to end at the other—everything is sculp-

MYRON. The discus thrower. Copy of the Greek. (*National Museum, Rome*).

tured from within, everything obeys inner forces in order to reveal their meaning to us. The living wave runs through the limbs, they are instinct with it, rounded or extended by it; it models the heads of the bones and, as ravines cut into a plain, it indents the glorious torsos from the secret belly to the tremble of the hard breasts. The sap, which rises in it and causes it to pulsate, makes of each fragment of the material, even when broken, a moving entity which participates in the existence of the whole, receiving life from it and returning life to it. An organic solidarity binds the parts together triumphantly. A higher life of the soul, for the first and the only time in history merged and confounded with the tempestuous life of the elements, rises above a world intoxicated and strong in the immortal youth of a moment which cannot last.

From the dusk of morning to the dusk of night the pediments spread out their scroll of life. In them peace descends with the night and light mounts with the day. From the two arms of Phœbus, which emerge from the horizon, stretching out toward the peak of the world, to the head of the horse whose body is already in the shadow at the other side of the sky, life grows, marches on without haste, and diminishes. The whole of life. Without interruption these forms continue one another. Like peaceful vegetation they come forth from the earth and, in the air from which they draw their life, unite their branches and mingle their foliage. Alone or entwined, they continue one another, as the plain into which the hill melts, the valley that reaches up to the mountain, the river and its estuary which the sea absorbs and the bay which goes from promontory to promontory. The shoulder is made for the brow which lies on it, the arm for the waist which it embraces, the ground

Sicily (v Century). Temple of Segesta.

lends its strength to the hand that presses on it, to the arm that shoots up from it like a rough tree and that holds up the half-reclining torso. It is limitless space that goes to mingle with the blood in the breasts and, when one looks at the eyes one would say that at the depths of their motionless pools space weds with the spirit which has come to repose there and to recover its vigor. The mechanical course of the heavenly bodies, the sound of the sea, the eternal tide of its embryos, and the unseizable flight of universal movement pass incessantly into these profound forms to blossom into intelligent energy.

A great and solemn moment! Man prolongs nature, whose rhythm is in his heart, determining, at each beat, the flux and reflux of his soul. Consciousness explains instinct and fulfills its higher function, which is to penetrate the order of the world, that it may obey it the better. The soul consents not to abandon the form, but to express itself through the form, and to let its single light flash out at the contact. The mind is like the perfume of man's necessary sensualism, and the senses demand of the mind that it justify their desires. Reason does not yet weaken sentiment; instead sentiment acquires new strength by marrying with reason. The highest idealism never loses sight of the actual elements of its generalizations, and when the Greek artist models a form in nature it shines with a spontaneous light of symbolic truth.

Greek art, at this time, reaches the philosophic moment. It is a thing of living change. Idealistic in its desire, it lives because it demands of life the elements of its ideal constructions. It is the species in the law, the man and the woman, the horse and the ox, the flower, the fruit, the being exclusively described by its essential qualities and made to live as it is, in the exercise of its normal functions. It is, at the same time, a man, a horse, an ox, a flower, and a fruit. The great Venus, peaceful as an absolute, is willed by the whole race. She sums up its hopes, she fixes its desire, but her swelling neck, her beautiful ripening breasts, her moving sides make her alive. She lends her glow

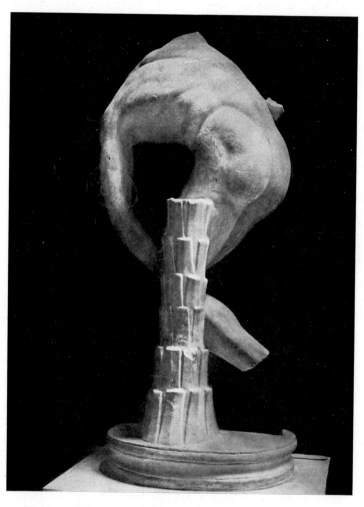

MYRON. The discus thrower. Fragment of a Greek copy
(*National Museum, Rome*).

to space which caresses her, touches her sides with gold, makes her lungs rise and fall. It penetrates her, she mingles with it. She is the unseizable instant when eternity meets universal life.

This state of equilibrium, wherein all the vital powers seem to hang suspended in the consciousness of man before bursting forth and multiplying under definite forms, imparts its force to all Greek art of the highest class. The anonymous sculptor of Olympia and Phidias and his pupils, the architects of the Acropolis, express the same relations, the same prodigious and blended universe brought to the human scale, the same type of reason, superior to the accidents of nature and subordinated to its laws. But the language of each one remains as personal as his body, his hands, the form of his forehead, the color of his eyes, the whole of his elemental substance, which is written into the marble by the same stroke that renders the universal order which he has understood and marked with its external form. See the faith, the almost savage sweep of the man who made the statues of Olympia, his rugged and broad phrase. See the religion, the sustained energy, the reserve of Phidias, his long, balanced phrase. See, in the encircling frieze, the discretion of his pupils who have neither his freedom nor his power, but who are calm as he is, because, like him, they live in an hour of certitude. Man, the animals, and the elements, everything consents to its role, and the artist feels, in his fraternal heart, the joy of this consent. It is with the same spirit that he tells of the warmth of women, the strength of men, and the rumination of oxen. A life as glorious as the summer! Man has seized the meaning of his activity; it is by what is around him that he frees himself and cultivates himself; it is through himself that he humanizes what is around him.

PHIDIAS (?), (about 440 B.C.). Tympanum of the Parthenon. The horse of night (*British Museum*).

The bad Roman copies of works belonging to the last period of Greece, the soft goddesses, the draped gods brandishing their lyres, the figures from literature and works of the school have for a long time calumniated Greek art. It expressed to us a colorless people, assuming a theatrical attitude to overawe the future. The artificial heroism hid the real heroism, and the ruggedness and freshness of the primitive were effaced by the fictions of the Alexandrine romancers. We used to describe the draperies of the "Fates" before having seen their knees, the shelter of their warm abdomen, and their torsos mounting with the power

PHIDIAS (?), (about 440 B.C.). Tympanum of the Parthenon. Theseus (*British Museum*).

and tumult of a wave to the absent heads which we divine as leaning over in confidences and confession. The anatomy of the "Theseus" and the "Ilyssus" masked the formidable life that swells and dilates them and makes its pulsations pass even to the fragments that have disappeared. The "Panatheniac Frieze" revealed to us the manner in which girls walk as they bear burdens, flowers, and sheaves, how horsemen defile, the tranquillity of intelligent strength dominating brute strength, how oxen go with the same step to the slaughterhouse and to work. We had forgotten that these were men and women who had lived, who had loved and suffered, and beasts which used to dig the furrows in the thin plain of Attica, and whose fat and flesh used to burn on the altars.

PHIDIAS (?), (about 440 B.C.). Tympanum of the Parthenon. The Fates, detail (*British Museum*).

Whether the mutilated marbles which carry Greek thought from the frontiers of archaism to the threshold of the decadence are wrestlers or virgins, the ease of strength shines from them, and an irresistible sweetness. When we come forth from the murderous effigies of Assyria or the silent statues of Egypt we feel ourselves brought back into the living universe, after having attuned the primitive instincts to the world of the mind. The obsessing anguish and the terror retreat into memory; we breathe deeply, we find ourselves to be what we did not yet know we were; we are the beings imaged by our presentiments.

Ictinos. The Parthenon (447-432), Athens.

We have seen the athletes arise quite naked in the light, as numerous as the old beliefs, and the young, astonished faces starting from the blue and green robes, like great flowers amid the fields. Demeter has left the ruins of Eleusis, tenderly to place in the hand of the calm Triptolemus the grain of wheat which is to give bread to men, and with it, science and peace. Blind desire and divine modesty, the eternal conflict that compromises or realizes our higher equilibrium—all this we have seen issuing from the dust of Olympia, with the brutes in their madness, the virgins assailed,

NEMEA (v Century). Temple of Zeus.

their beautiful bodies that struggle out of the embrace, their beautiful heavy arms in revolt. There, at the level of the ground, we have picked up the trace of the life of the little slaves of the old serving-woman,

PHIDIAS (school of), (about 440 B.C.). The Parthenon. Horsemen of the Frieze (*British Museum*).

and, at the angle of the pediments, we have felt the weight of the breast of women already feeling the movement of new life within them. With the good Herakles, we have carried the globe, swept the stable, and strangled the monsters; we have wandered over the earth to make it healthful, and our hearts with it. In the pediments of the great temple of the Acropolis, with the rough-grained torsos, the full limbs, the wave of humanity that mounts and is appeased, we have recognized, in the projections into the light and the hollowings into the shadow, the image of our destiny. The panting Victories have hung upon their wings that we may surprise, under the robe that proclaims it, the hesitation of the flanks, the breasts, the belly, as they emerge into their prime. All these deified beings show us at once the roots and the summit of our effort.

IV

The meeting of life and of the accessible heavens, this ideal realized on the face of the temples and in the intelligence of the heroes, was to flower, for the glory of the Greeks and the demonstration of the unity of the soul, on a

ATTIC ART. Apollo (*Louvre*).

political plane of struggle and liberation. Democracy is not fully victorious and consequently it is already on the road to decline, but Greece makes the effort from which democracy is to be born. With the wooden idols and the multicolored monsters of the old temples came the death of the oligarchy, the power delegated to a caste which, at bottom, symbolized accepted revelation. Tyranny, which, in Greece, is government by one man whose science has been recognized, the system whose apogee coincides, in the fourth century, with the determination of sculptural science—tyranny is shaken when the movement of life invades the archaic form. The first statues to stir are those of Harmodios and Aristogiton, the men who killed the King of Athens. Then the crushing forces which Æschylus set like blocks upon the human soul are shaken, with Sophocles, to penetrate one another, to act on one another, and to cause their balanced energy to radiate in consciousness and will. Then Phidias transports into marble the poise of life, and man is ripe for liberty. Democracy appears—the transitory political expression of the antagonism and the agreement of forces in the cosmic harmony.

Then from every Acropolis a Parthenon arises. The chief of the democracy inspires them, the people work at them, the humblest stonecutter gets the same pay as Ictinos the architect, or Phidias the sculptor. At the Panatheniac festivals, with the ritual order ill observed by the enthusiastic populace, in the dust and the sunlight, to the often discordant sound of Oriental music and the thousand bare feet striking the ground, with the brutal splendor of the dyed robes, the jewels, the rouge, and the fruits, the city sends to the Parthenon its hope—with the young girls scattering flowers, waving palms, and singing hymns, its strength with the horsemen, and its wisdom with the old men. The protecting divinity is to be thanked for having permitted the meeting and sanctioned the accord between man and the law.

The temple sums up the Greek soul. It is neither the house of the priest as the Egyptian temple was,

Phidias (?), Ionian school (?). Young priestess
(*National Museum, Rome*).

nor the house of the people as the cathedral is to be; it is the house of the spirit, the symbolic refuge where the wedding of the senses and the will is to be celebrated. The statues, the paintings—all the plastic effort of the intelligence—is used to decorate it. The

ATHENS (about 415 B.C.). Erechteion, portico of the Caryatids, detail.

detail of its construction is the personal language of the architect. Its principle is always the same, its proportions are always similar, it is the same spirit that calculates and balances its lines. Here the Doric genius dominates, by the austere unornamented column, broad and short; there the Ionic genius smiles in it, through the long column, graceful as a jet of water and gently expanded at its summit. Some-

ATHENS (end of v Century). Victory, fragment of the balustrade of the temple of Athena Nike (*Museum of the Acropolis*).

times young girls, inclining toward one another as they walk, balance the architrave on their heads, like a basket of fruit. Often it has columns on only one or two faces; at other times they surround it entirely. Whether it is large or small, its size is never thought of. We are tempted to say that the law of Number, which it observes with such ease, is innate with it; one would say that the law springs from this very soil as the shafts rise in their vertical flight between the stylobate and the architrave, that it is the law itself which halts them, and which hangs suspended in the pediment with a sort of motionless balance. The law of Number easily places the temple in the scale of the material and spiritual universe of which it is the complete expression. It is on a plane with the pure gulf which, at its base, rounds a curve formed by the cadenced wave that comes to sweep the blond sand. It is on a plane with its own promontory, which turns violet or mauve according to the hour, but is always defined against space by a continuous line, which the bony structure of the earth marks out distinctly. It is on a plane with the day sky, which outlines the regularity of its rectangle in the ring of the horizon of the sea. It is on a plane with the night sky which turns about it according to the musical and monotonous rhythm in which the architect has discovered the secret of its proportions. It is on a plane with the city, for which it realizes, with a strange serenity, the perfect equilibrium vainly sought by its citizens in the essential antagonism of classes and parties.

It is on a plane with the poets and thinkers, who

seek the absolute relationship between the heart and the intelligence in tragedy and dialogue, to which it is related by the drama of its sculptural decoration, irrevocably inscribed in its definite order. On the

ATHENS (end of the v Century). Temple of the Wingless Victory.

simple Acropolis it is a harmony that crowns another harmony. After twenty-five centuries it remains what it was, because it has retained its proportions, its sustained sweep, its strong seat on the great slabs of stone that dominate the sea surrounded by golden hills. One might say that the years have treated it as they have treated the earth, despoiling it of its statues and of its colors at the same time that they have carried the forests and the soil of the mountains down to the sea and dried up the torrents. One might say that the years have burned it as they have burned the skeleton of the soil which crops out everywhere under the reddish grass—that eight hundred thousand days of flame have penetrated it to make it tower over the conflagration of the evening, seeming to mount even higher the lower the sun descends.

If one has not lived in the intimacy of its ruins, one thinks the Greek temple as rigid as a theorem. But as soon as we really know it—whether almost intact or shattered—our whole humanity trembles in it. The reason is that from its base to its summit the theorem bears the trace of the hand. As in the pediments, the symmetry is only apparent, but equilibrium reigns and makes it live. The laws of sculpture, the laws of nature, are found in it, with logic, the energy and silence of the planes, the quiver of their surfaces. The straight line is there, as solid as reason, the spacious curved line also, reposeful as the dream. The architect secures the stability of the edifice by its rectangular forms, he gives it movement by its hidden curves. The sweep of the columns is oblique; they project a little, one beyond the other, like the trees of an avenue. An insensible curve rounds off the architrave at the line of their summit. All these imperceptible divergences, with the fluting of the columns—a shell which breaks the light, a stream of shadow and of fire—animate the temple, give to it something like the beating of a heart. Its pillars possess the strength and the tremor of trees; the pediments and the friezes oscillate like the branches. The edifice, hidden behind the curtain of the columns, resembles the mysterious

DELPHI (end of the v Century). Capital of the dancers (*Museum of Delphi*).

forest which opens at the moment one enters it. The temple of Pæstum, which is quite black, has the appearance of an animal walking.

Thus, from the living temple to the eternal men who people its pediments and march in the circle of its friezes, Greek art is a melody. Man's action is fused with his thought. Art comes from him, as does his glance, his voice, and his breath, in a kind of conscious enthusiasm; which is the true religion. So lucid a faith exalts him that he has no need to cry it forth. His lyrism is contained, because he knows the reason of its existence. His certitude is that of the regular force which causes torrents of desire and the flowers to spring from beings and from the soil. And the Apollo, who arises from the pediment of Olympia with the calm and the sweep of the sun as it passes the horizon, and whose resplendent gesture dominates the fury of the crowds, is like the spirit of this race which, for a second, felt the reign over the chaos that surrounds us, of the order inherent within us.

A second! no longer, doubtless, and we cannot determine its place. It is mysterious, it escapes our attempt to measure it, as do all human works in which intuition plays the larger part. Did it perhaps burst out in a lost work, perhaps in several works at once? Toward the middle of the fifth century, from the sculptor of Olympia to Phidias, between the rise and the fall, there occurs in the whole soul of Greece an immense oscillation round about this unseizable moment, which passed without her being able to retain it. But she lived it, and one or two men

PHIDIAS

expressed it. And that is the maximum that a living humanity has a right to demand of the dead humanities. It is not by following them that it will resemble them. It may seek and discover in itself the elements of a new equilibrium. But a mode of equilibrium cannot be rediscovered.

Hypnos (?), (v to iv Centuries?). (*Perugia.*)

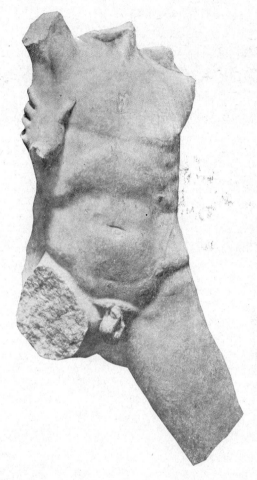

POLYCLEITUS (school of). Torso of a man fighting.

The Acropolis of Pergamum.

Chapter VI. THE DUSK OF MANKIND

I

HE heroic soul of Greece was to ebb away through three wounds: the triumph of Sparta, the enr chment of Athens, and the reign of intellectualism. Sensibility increased at the expense of moral energy, reason overflowed faith, enthusiasm was dulled through contact with the critical spirit. The philosophers, to whose development sculpture had contributed so much by giving life to ideas, were to deny their origin, laugh at the poets and at the artists, and discourage the sculptors through misleading their minds in the meanders of sophistry. We need not bear them a grudge for this. The equilibrium was about to break; no human power, no miracle could have re-established it.

And the soul of Athens, on the brink of the abyss to which her logicians were dragging civilization, was even then forging a tool with which the men of a distant future could build a new dwelling. The death struggle of Greece gave us freedom of examination.

Beginning with the last years of the fifth century, a furtive caress passed over the Greek marbles. The great forms, kept alive by the circulation of their inner energies, disappeared from the pediments, and the artist tried to call these energies to the surface of the statues, of the portraits, of the picturesque groups which, however, he isolated little by little. The form and the spirit, which up to that time had flowered in the same integral expression, now separated from each other irrevocably. The spiritualist searched the body to extract the soul, the skeptic no longer tried to derive from it anything more than sensual satisfactions. About that time a little temple was built on the Acropolis to house a wingless Victory. But the external victories that had descended upon it had kept their wings. They were to depart from Athens.

Greek sculpture is supposed not to have appreciated the inner life until the fourth century. It might be observed that from the Archaic period onward there are statues, like the Samian woman, or like any Orante of the Acropolis, whose visage makes us think of that of the Gothic virgins because of their naïve enchantment with life which illumines it from within. But that is not the question. People generally believe that thought cannot dwell anywhere save in the head

EPIDAURUS (beginning of the IV Century B.C.). Victory of the Acroterium of the temple of Esculapius (*National Museum, Athens*).

of the model. The truth is that it is entirely in the head of the artist. The inner quality of a work is measured by the quality of the relations which unite its elements and assure the continuity of its ensemble. And no art had more of the inner quality than that of the fifth century. The modeling of everything goes from within outward. The surfaces, the movements, the empty spaces themselves, everything is determined by the play of the profound forces that pass from the artist into the material, as the blood passes from the heart into the limbs and the brain.

PRAXITELES (end of IV Century). Hermes, detail (*Museum of Olympia*).

It is true that in a poor society, where the slave was well treated, where the steps of the social hierarchy were very near together, one which lived on an indulgent soil, in a health-giving air, near a flowered sea, human beings did not have an urgent need of one another. The normal expression of man is a resultant of the daily conflict of his passions and his will. The Greek sculptor knew the sentimental agitations whose reflections pass at times over the sternest among human faces. But it was only later, with the definitive breaking of the social rhythm, that these reflections

LYSIPPUS (school of). Ephebe, bronze, detail (*National Museum, Athens*).

were imprinted there as indelible traces. Man, who was then to be characterized by a warped, suffering body and a haggard face, was defined for Phidias by a complete organic equilibrium wherein the calm of the heart spread through the harmony of the general structure, of which the tranquil face was only one

Scopas (352). The Mausoleum, detail (*British Museum*).

element. The head of the Lapith woman, that of Peitho, and that of the Artemis of the Parthenon express a profound life, but a peaceful one. It is like a great depth of pure water, full and limpid and unruffled. The world does not yet know water forever plowed by the storm, blackened by the poisonous miasmas that slept in it.

Praxiteles draws the spirit to the skin of the statues. As he sees the spirit floating on faces as an undefined smile, as a vague disquietude, as a luminous shadow, he fixes it there, and by so doing breaks that unity

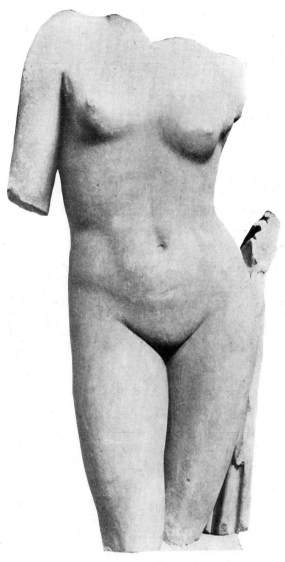

PRAXITELES (school of), (end of the IV Century).
Aphrodite (*Museum of Naples*).

which gives to the forms of the great century their contained radiance. To express the inner life he seeks to make it external. And it is no longer as a dawn, it is as an evening, that the soul mounts from the depths to spread itself over the surface. Praxiteles is the Euripides of sculpture. His measure, his elegance, his mind, the subtlety of his animation, and the charm of his analysis do not succeed in hiding from us the fact that he doubts his strength, and that, at bottom, he regrets having lost the sacred intoxication at which he laughs. Under his fingers the plane gets soft, hesitates, and gradually loses the spiritual energy with which Phidias invested it. The expression of the form, distraught and as if a little wearied, is no longer the play of the inner forces, but that of the lights and shadows on its shell. The soul seeks to escape from the embrace of the marble. One sees this clearly in the great dreamy foreheads under the wavy hair, in the sensual and vibrant mouth, in the undefined charm of the face as it leans forward. That no longer means intelligence; that means sentiment. Art dies of it, but new life takes its germ from it and, much later and under other skies, is to flower from it. At the moment when human language and enthusiasm weaken together, the work of Praxiteles affirms, not the appearance, but the survival of the mind and a kind of transference of its function, which is to spend many long centuries in searching for its real organ and in the end is to find it.

His art betrays the coming of a kind of cerebral sensualism which we see appearing at the same hour

THE DUSK OF MANKIND

among all his contemporaries, to whom the friezes of the temple of the "Wingless Victory" and the capital of the "Dancers" at Delphi had already shown the way. Little by little, the deep structure is forgotten,

Niobide, copy (IV to III Century B.C.).
(*Banque Commerciale, Rome.*)

so that the surface of the figures may be caressed by desire, as the surface of the faces is marked by the artist's effort to depict psychological states. When the statue remains clothed, the robes become lighter than a breeze on the water. But, for the first time, the Greek sculptor wholly unveils woman, whose form is significant more especially through the tremor of its surface, just as the masculine form, which had dictated his science to him, is above all significant through the logic and the rigor of its structure. For the first time he rejects the stuffs which the pupils of Phidias had begun to drape in every direction, at the risk of leaving unexpressed the life moving under them. It is without veils that he expresses the movement of the torsos as they draw themselves up to their full stature, the animation of the planes which the light and air model in powerful vibration, the youth of breasts, the vigor of masculine bellies, and the pure thrust of arms and legs. He speaks of the body of woman as it had never been spoken of before, he raises it up and adores it in its radiant warmth, its firm undulations, in its splendor as a living column through which the sap of the world circulates with its blood. These mutilated statues confer on the sensuality of man the highest nobility. Full and pure, like a well of light, intrusted by all their profiles to space which is motionless about them, as if filled with respect, these great forms sanctify the whole of paganism as, later, a mother bending over the dead body of her son is to humanize Christianity. And if we are intimately grateful to Praxiteles and regard him with a tenderness which does not resemble the heroic exaltation to which Phidias transports us, it is because he has taught us that the feminine body, by its rise into the light and the affecting frailty of the belly, the sides, and the breasts in which our whole

THE DUSK OF MANKIND

future sleeps, sums up human effort in the unconquerable idealism with which it faces so many storms. It is impossible to see certain of these broken statues where only the young torso and the long thighs survive, without being torn by a tenderness that is sacred.

II

But the early fervor is soon to be transformed; something a little wearied is to touch the force of the marble. Very quickly the forms lengthen, become more slender, flow like a single caress, and tremble with sensual agitation, with shame invaded by love. The modeling undulates gently, the *passage* becomes insistent, insinuates itself, and, little by little, effaces the plane. Wandering hollows dapple the skin, the breasts are uncertain flowers which never quite open, the neck swells as if with sighs, the knot of hair secured by the fillets weighs on the beautiful round head over which the tresses course like a stream. As at the end of Egypt, it is the troubled farewell to woman, a farewell in which sleeps the hope of distant resurrections. Look, after seeing the "Victories," after the "Dancers" of Delphi—so natural in their grace that they make one think of a tuft of reeds—look at the "Leda" as she stands to receive the great swan with the beating wings, letting the beak seize her neck, the foot tighten on her thigh—the trembling woman subjected to the fatal force which reveals to her the whole of life, even while penetrating her with voluptuousness and pain. And that is still religious, grave, barely infected by heady agitation, barely turning towards the slope of sensual abandon—it is like the adieu of Greece to the noble life of the pagans. The heroic era of paganism

MAGNA GRÆCIA (end of the IV Century). Psyche of Capua (*Museum of Naples*).

begins its death struggle with a smile that is a little melancholy, but tender and resigned. It seems as if this admirable race had had a feeling of the rela-

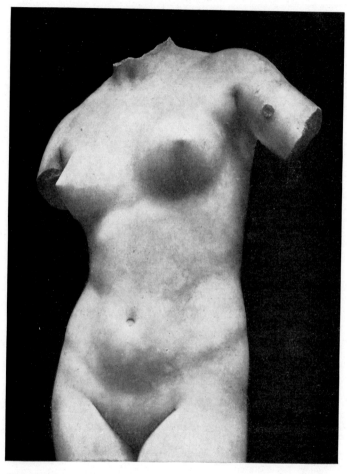

HELLENISTIC ART (IV to III Centuries). Aphrodite of Cyrene, detail (*National Museum, Rome*).

tivity of our knowledge and as if it had accepted the beginning of its decline as simply as it had accepted its dawn.

Thus, through criticism and sensuality, Greece came to study the actual man and to forget the possible man. Lysippus began again to cast athletes in bronze, muscular and calm young men, whose immediate life, no longer the inner one, goes no deeper than their rippling skin. The form, indeed, is always full and pure; it is dense and unsettled, but coherent, and has the look of a thing conceived as a whole. When these athletes left the stadium they seemed to descend from the temple, so well did the serenity, the assurance of their strength, still concentrate in them. But the hieratic idea of the first periods of sculpture, the divine idea of the great century, no longer interposed between them and the statue maker, who saw them directly. At the same time and by the same means he turned his sculpture toward those character portraits which, in reality, we know only by the Roman copies. The earlier ones—that of Homer, for example—reveal to us disenchanted nobility, discriminating fineness and reserve. But later we find fever, excessive sensitiveness, and virtuosity in description. It is a movement, moreover, which announces the gravest social crisis. Art is no longer a function of the race; it begins to make itself dependent on the rich man, who is to turn it away from its heroic course more and more, to demand of it portraits and statues for apartments and gardens.

The last of the great monuments of the classic epoch,

the Mausoleum of Scopas and Bryaxis, is made for a private individual, King Mausolus, and, by an irony which partakes of the symbolic, this monument is a

HELLENISTIC ART (IV to III Century). Aphrodite of Zonaglia (*Louvre*).

tomb. It is living, certainly—nervous, sparkling, and impregnated with intelligence. In the warriors, in the Amazons and their horses, in the races, the flights, and the attacks, there circulates a free, proud, and delicate spirit, a rapidity of thought which almost forestalls the action, which brings into the material the resonance of the armor, the neighing of the horses, the sound of their hoofs beating on the ground, and of the vibrations of javelins and tightly drawn bowstrings. The chisel attacks the marble with the conquering fire of a too ardent mind in anxious haste to set down at the flood tide of its excitation, an enthusiasm already tainted with doubt. With its extreme elegance of form, its sharp mordant expression, and its direct gesture, it is a cool breeze that crosses an early evening. There are constant parallelisms between fold and fold, between limb and limb, between movement and movement. The empty spaces are very empty, we no longer feel the passage of that abstract wave through which the volumes penetrated one another and, from end to end of the pediment, gave the effect of a sea whose crests brought with them the hollows—which heave to a crest again. The hollow is isolated here, the wave is isolated; picturesque and descriptive detail profits by this dissociation to appear and impose itself. It is to tend, more and more, to predominate over the philosophic ensemble.

The evolution of the great periods is approximately the same everywhere; but in Greece from the seventh to the third century it appears with an astonishing relief. Man, when he realizes himself, proceeds like nature, from anarchy to unity, from unity to anarchy. At first the scattered elements have to seek one another in the darkness of the mind. Then the whole mass of the chaotic creature is weighed down by the soil, which clogs its joints and clings to its heavy steps. Then the forms disengage themselves and find their proper places and agreement; their logical relationships appear, and each organ adapts itself more and more closely to its function. In the end the rhythm is

Homer, bronze
(*Archæological Museum, Florence*).

broken, form seems to flee from form, the mind seems to wander at random, the contacts are lost, the unity disintegrates. Thus there are in Greek art four definite epochs: the Primitives, Ægina, the Parthenon, the Mausoleum. First, the stammering analysis followed, with the Archaic men, by a brief and rough synthesis. Then, when the mind is mature, a new and short analysis, luminous and compelling, which ends, with a single bound, in the conscious synthesis of a society in equilibrium. Finally, a last research which is not to reach its goal, which is to dissipate itself more and more until it has reduced its fragments *ad infinitum*, has broken all the old bonds, and has, little by little, lost itself through lack of comprehension, fatigue, and the urgent need of a great, new power of feeling.

His forgetting of the essential relations causes the artist to become concerned over the accident, the rare movement, the exceptional expression, the momentary action and, most of all—when men turn back to the horizon of the mystical, the artist's solicitude takes the form of looking for fright, pain, delirium, for physical suffering, and sentimental impulses of all kinds. The plastic synthesis undergoes the same disintegration. It is then that detail appears; it tyrannizes over the artist. The attribute invades the form. The latter gesticulates in vain as if it wanted to defend itself, the attribute rivets itself on like a chain. Lyres, tridents, scepters, lightnings, draperies, sandals, headdresses—the whole rag bag of the studios and the theatrical dressing-room makes its entrance. The deep lyrism of the soul subsides, there is need for an external lyrism to mask its exhaustion. It was enthusiasm that made the statue divine; how is the god to be recognized now if he has no scepter and no crown? Faith uplifted the material and made lightning flash from it to the very heavens of human hope. That is over with. The statues need wings. In the fifth century the wing was rare on the shoulders of the gods. It was to be found among the Archaics as they tried to tear form from the chains of matter. It

Demeter of Cnidus (end of IV Century). (*British Museum.*)

is found among the decadents where it tries to raise the form, whose own ardor no longer sustains it. The "Victory of Samothrace" already has need of wings to rise from the prow of the ship, because of the

HELLENISTIC ART (III Century B.C.). Sarcophagus of Alexander (*Museum of Constantinople*).

complication of the wet draperies which weigh on her legs and make heavy her terrible sweep, the turn of her bust, and the tempest of flight, of clarions, and of the wind that rises in her wake.

III

Greek art, at the very moment that it was thus breaking up in depth, was scattering over the whole material surface of Hellenic antiquity. After the movement of concentration that had brought to Athens all the forces of Hellenism, a movement of dispersal began, which was to carry from Athens to southern Italy, to Sicily, to Cyrenaica, Egypt, the Islands, and Asia Minor the passion and, unfortunately, the mania, for beautiful things—in default of creative

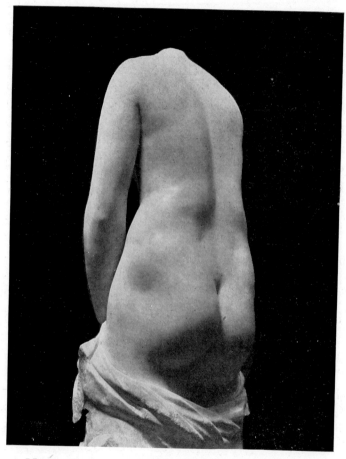

Magna Græcia (III Century B.C.). Aphrodite, detail (*Museum of Syracuse*).

genius. Dilettantism and the diffusion of taste multiply and at the same time weaken talent. It is the Hellenistic period, perhaps the richest in artists and in works of art that history has to show, but perhaps, also, one of the poorest in power of emotion.

There are few men to listen to the voice within them now, and, in a brief rush of fervor, occasionally to catch from it—like the vigorous sculptor of the Venus of Milo—a very noble, if somewhat dulled and disunited, echo of the hymn to life whose triumphal choir dies out in the past. The adroit and active author of the "Sarcophagus of Alexander" takes the subjects of the old Assyrian sculpture, for lack of its science, and transforms its force and its brutality into somewhat declamatory lyrical movement. The sculptors of Rhodes, especially, seek gesticulating and complicated melodrama in the sensational event and in literature, so that they may be surer to touch popular sentiment, which is beginning its reaction against the skepticism of the philosophers. Others, who cannot see significance in the normal manifestations of life, lure the patron by making their work tell anecdotes for him. We reach the irritating reign of the picturesque little groups. They are still charming sculpture, to be sure, of a learned and witty elegance, but without the naïve quality, and already announce monotonous factory work, trinkets, art for the amateur, and those coffins of the artist's dignity, the glass case, the shelf, and the collection.

These undefined currents, dominated by the sentimentalism of the middle classes and the elegant lassitude of the blasé, act one on another, in harmony or in opposition, and follow or push back in every direction the hesitating wave that goes from the shores of Asia to the shores of Egypt, from Pergamos to Alex-

Sleeping Fury (III Century B.C.).
(*National Museum, Rome.*)

andria, from the Islands to the three continents. The incessant mixing of the populations of the coasts produces a wild maelstrom in which some waves from the depths, bringing back the violence and heaviness of Asia, arouse the passion of humanity to the point of desperation. But the Greek soul is no longer anything but a foam evaporating on the surface. Man has lost his unity. His efforts to seize it again only plunge him into deeper night. The *Altar* of Pergamos, the last of the great collective designs that Hellenism has bequeathed to us, is the image of this disorder. Where sobriety had been, there is heavy luxuriance; confusion replaces order; the rhythm grows wild and breathless; melodramatic effort stifles all humanity, and oratorical power becomes emphasis and bombast. The artist, in the abundance of his speech, exhibits the noisy emptiness of his mind. His speech is ardent, without doubt, sumptuous in color, trembling with his clamor and his gesture, but it is a little like a mantle loaded with gold and gems that has been caught by the wind. Scopas had, at least, no fear of open spaces in his groups; he was too much alive; the sap of the primitive had not abandoned him; when he had nothing to say he held his peace. But the sculptor of Pergamos is afraid of those great silences through which the spirit of Phidias, when it left one form to go toward another, glided on its invisible wave. The sense of spiritual continuity is so foreign to him that he does not hesitate to replace it by the factitious continuity of external rhetoric. He fills the backgrounds, stuffs the holes, and chokes up every bit of space that he can find. When a man has little to say, he talks without a stop. Silence bores only those who do not think.

These screams, these imploring eyes, these desperate gestures correspond with the awakening neither of pain nor of pity. Suffering is as old as the mind. The men of the past were not ignorant of the dramas of love, or the dramas of paternity, or the dramas of war, or of abandonment, or of death; but they knew how

THE DUSK OF MANKIND

to gather from them an increase of power. When man loves life he dominates and utilizes pain. It is when he no longer acts that tears rule the world. The lachrymose heroes and the epileptic gods no longer have in them anything of the Greek soul; they no

PERGAMUM (beginning of the II Century). Altar (*Museum of Berlin*).

longer have anything of the human soul. It escapes through the bellowing mouths, the hair standing on end, the tips of the fingers, the points of the spears, and through the gestures that fritter it away. The world is ripe to adopt the antagonistic dualism that later is to tear civilization to pieces. Here is earth, there is heaven; here is the form, there is the spirit. They are forbidden to rejoin each other, to recognize themselves in each other. Man is to wander despairingly for ten or twelve centuries in the night that falls between them. Already the authors of the melodramatic groups of the "Laocoon," the "Farnese Bull," and the romantic suicides are no longer sculptors, but bombastic play-actors. Feeling, which is to be reborn in the crowds, is dead in the image cutters, who have been domesticated by the powerful. Even their science is dead. The statue maker is hardly more than a diligent anatomist, who follows exactly the relief of the muscles and the dramatized movement that fashion prescribes for his model. Sculpture does not even think of recovering something of the lost paradise through divine irony, for which it is not made. But through irony Lucian of Samosate is to console minds from which pitiless rationalism has driven out faith. The gods have deserted the souls of the artists to dwell in the hearts of stoics, who welcome them without a word.

IV

There is to be, indeed, during this slow, irremediable wasting away of the Greek idea, some moments where the decline is arrested, some startled gestures revealing a momentary return of vitality; occasionally a few green shoots come from the old transplanted tree. Nothing dies without a struggle. Upon coming into contact with newer races, the Hellenic genius, ashamed of its decay, attempts a vigorous return to itself here and there, and if it does not bring the gods back to earth, it sees, living on the earth, a few heroic forms around the flourishing cities and the illumined bays. To follow its infiltrations through the Latins of northern Italy and the Latinized colonies of the valley of the Rhone is rather difficult, the more so because, from the

DAMOPHON (beginning of the II Century). Artemis of Lycosoura (*National Museum, Athens*).

origins of Greek civilization, Magna Græcia had not ceased to cultivate thought, to cut marble, and to cast bronze. Pæstum in its swamps, and the temples of Sicily on their soil of lava and sulphur, where the herds of goats wander amid the cactus, bear witness to the fact that a collective power reigned. It was triumphant over wars, it defined the idealism of the race even more than it did the character of the cities. The evolution of the Hellenic desire had been everywhere the same. Magna Græcia had bared its goddesses to discover the woman in them at the same moment that Praxiteles had. But perhaps it had grown soft more quickly, as if submerged in voluptuous and enervating luxury. Southern Italy was richer than Greece, more fertile, less rugged, and more generously supplied with orange trees, with flowers, and with breezes. The beautiful statues of Capua have the fluidity of perfumed oils and the polish of the skin of courtesans; they are without any strength of their own, their modeling melts and flows like wax. Rome had little trouble in subjecting those who lived among them.

But it happened that at the contact of Roman energy the Greek element recovered a certain dignity. For two centuries, approximately, from the period when Greece, not yet conquered, but already resigned, sent artists to Rome, until the period when, entirely vanquished, she furnished only panderers, sophists, and rhetoricians—from the "Seated Pugilist" to the "Hercules of the Belvedere"—there was a strange union of the violent Latin strength and the Hellenic

THE DUSK OF MANKIND

mind, purified and made subtle by the approach of death. And from this marriage came fruits at once so tart and so ripe that before them Michael Angelo

MYRINA. The Vintage, bas-relief (*Louvre*).

could have recognized—and did recognize—his power. These are singular works, like full green oaks that have been struck by lightning. We do not know whether they are Roman, because of the hilly modeling, the exaggerated expressiveness of the projections, and the tense brutality; or Greek, because of the mastery that fixes all these qualities in coherent form, that draws forth and distributes the spirit of the form.

The accord between the inner life of the recreated organism and its mode of meeting with the light on its surface is complete. In these works instinct is dominated by intelligence, and must follow wherever and

HELLENISTIC ART. Bacchus and Ariadne. Sarcophagus, fragment (*Louvre*).

however intelligence directs it. It was surely Latinized Greeks in Sicily who dug out from the rocks, which look toward the sparkling sea, those marble amphitheaters where the shepherds sat beside the gods. It was Latinized Greeks who built and decorated Pompeii. It was Latinized Greeks, saturated with that concrete poetry which the French soil infuses in those whom it nourishes, who built Arles

GRECO-ROMAN ART. Pugilist, bronze (II Century B.C.).
(*National Museum, Rome.*)

and Nîmes and surprised those beautiful women at the bath as they crouch on one leg which flattens under the weight of the torso, with its soft breasts, the fat fold at the belly, and the hollow in the small of the back, where the shadow moves with the undulating surface. At Rome itself, under Augustus, with the Roman copyists all around him, Pasiteles founded a Greek school. And it was in Rome, under his leadership and as an evident reaction against Asiatic sculpture, that the Greek sculptors attempted an impossible return to Archaic austerity.[1] Everywhere else, in Attica, in Asia, and in the Islands, Hellenism reacts in only a negative way against the sea of sentimentalism that arises from the depths.

V

But it still discusses, it wrangles, and, let us add, it tries, in the wreck of its spirit, to bequeathe the essential lesson of that spirit—if not by the language of form which it scarcely knows any longer, at least by words. About the first century the whole civiliza-

[1] I believe that the famous throne of Venus (of the Museo Nazionale in Rome), the central element of which serves as the headpiece to the Introduction to this book, and which has heretofore been attributed to the fifth century, must be restored to this school, of which it would be the masterpiece. Not to mention the place where it was discovered, not to speak of the nude figure in it—which, by the way, is inferior to the rest of the work—and which the artists of the fifth century would not have ventured to use, there are some strange details in it like the pillows, a certain negligence of style, a certain fashionable elegance, a certain technical cleverness, a spirit more elegant and refined than grave, a mixture of exquisite culture and voluntary naïveté, a shade of literature very far from the force and the austerity of the predecessors of Phidias.

THE DUSK OF MANKIND

tion of antiquity concentrates around Alexandria, as if to take an inventory of its conquests. The Egyptian, in his weariness, is at the back of the stage, but the

HELLENISTIC ART. Eros and Psyche (*Louvre*).

Jew and the Greek stand before the audience, applauded or hooted, friends or enemies. Now alone, now followed by fanatical multitudes, they work in the fever, the trepidation, and the clamor of a ceaselessly jostling and renewed cosmopolitanism. On a bed of abject vices, of intensified asceticisms, among uncompromising mystics and indulgent skeptics, the idea ferments. Philosophers, critics, romancers, theologians, rhetoricians, artists—this whole world mingles together and shouts. The artist goes in for theology, the philosopher for romances, the theologian for criticism, the romancer for rhetoric. It is a unique moment in the history of mankind; Egypt contributes its mystery, Greece its reason, Asia its god. And in spite of Egypt, Greece, and Asia, the synthesis of the ancient world, that is to be effected in the too aristocratic domain of the mind by the enthusiasm of the prophets and the subtlety of the sophists, is to pass over the mass of humanity without satisfying the hunger of its needs. The world is wearied with thinking, it tempers its unsettled ideal in its primitive element once more—in the innocence of the people. A new mythology is to triumph over the philosophers, who are preparing its unfolding.

Social surroundings such as these do not permit belief in a great Alexandrian art, which would have been lost. Neither strong architecture nor great sculpture reposes on systems, especially when the systems interpenetrate and vary incessantly. The source of plastic inspiration had dried up in the too complicated mind of the upper classes and had not yet appeared in the dark soul of the people. At Alexandria, as at other places, there were admirable renewals, spiritual leaps as straight as those of a dying flame, the gleams of a deep love. Certain bas-reliefs of Alexandrian, Greco-Latin,

GRECO-ROMAN ART, APOLLONIOS (I Century B.C.). Hercules of the Belvedere (*Museum of the Vatican*).

or Hellenistic origin—the matter is of little importance for the same spirit insinuates itself everywhere—certain bas-reliefs seize upon us through the liveliness and the grace—the joy rescued from intellectual pessimism, the ardent abandon to the intoxication of enjoyment through understanding, and of understanding through enjoyment. The fruit of the vineyard is ripe, the vintagers gather it, to the sound of flute and cymbals; they dance on the grapes. A long, long winter may come. The round of the dancers grows wilder, the hair of the women streams, their heaving bosoms and their legs are bared, the panthers creep through the shadows to lick up the blood that is to flow. But this epoch, in which Egyptian hieratism often comes to tempt the dying inspiration of the Greek, cultivates "genre" sculpture, which is the unmistakable mark, on the dust of the centuries, of baseness and vulgarity of mind. These sculptors surprise the questionable professions in their picturesque adventures; they tell little stories that make you laugh or cry. It is the Japanese bibelot, done with far less skill, or the clock-top of the lower middle classes of our century with far more skill and not much more wit. The greater part of the bas-reliefs exhibit the same tendencies, the often confused and overloaded anecdote, and a background of landscape as its setting. They show how sculpture was corrupted in the Ptolemaic periods by the studies and method of painters. And that is the most serious of the social indications that can be found in this art.

This need of fusing the two great modes of plastic

THE DUSK OF MANKIND

evocation had been appearing in Greece itself for at least three centuries. Praxiteles looked on form as a painter rather than as a sculptor; Lysippus, also, at times, and the sculptor of the "Tomb of Alexander," and especially the decorator of Pergamos. The great classic sculpture had indeed made use of painting, but as an accessory means, to give to the form, already living through its own structure, the superficial appearance of life. Under the broad, simple tones which covered the decorative ensembles and remained tranquil in the light, the sculptural plane persisted. On the contrary, in the fourth century, and very much more in the Hellenistic periods, pictorial expression

ALEXANDRIAN ART. Head of a woman (*Laffan Collection*).

tends to get along without form and to model the surfaces by the mysterious play of the lights, the shadows, the half-tones, and the diffused envelope of the air. It is still a legitimate process when it is practiced on bas-relief, but it is fatal to sculpture. Form must live in space by its own means, like the living being. The planes determined by its inner life are the exact criterion of the statue's success or failure in its contact with the outside atmosphere. An envelope is necessary only to the painter, since he transfers conventionally, to a flat surface, the materiality and the depth of space. If the sculptor incorporates an artificial atmosphere with form, the real atmosphere will devour it.

In the epoch of Alexandria the confusion is complete. The mystics of Asia and the skeptics of Europe, wearied by their skepticism, need the vague envelope that destroys form and opens dreams as vague as itself. The great sculpture of Egypt, even while retaining its strong traditions, had already, in the Saite epoch, headed for these cloudy horizons. The anecdote surrounded by the mystery of painting, indeed the whole of Greek art from Praxiteles onward, tends toward them. Grandeur of sentiment having disappeared, sentimentalism, a new thing, was bound to germinate in the pain of the masses and the indecision of the intellectuals, to renew the energy of the world. It is only in these tendencies that we can find in Alexandrian art an attempt, even if an obscure one, to fuse the essential aspirations of the ideals of the ancient world.

The ideal of the Jew is justice. It is a limited and exclusive ideal, and, for that reason, uncompromising and hard. Like every excess of passion, the passion for justice, when it has no counterpoise, renders man unjust toward those who do not think as he does, and unjust toward himself, for his thought knows no other refuge than daily sacrifice and pitiless severity. He is unhappy and alone, for he is unacquainted with forgiveness. The ideal of the Greek is wisdom, the order of the world obeyed and disciplined by the intelligence, the conquest—patient and undivorced from

GALLO-HELLENIC ART (I Century A.D.). Crouching Venus (*Louvre*).

life—of a relative equilibrium. He has a strong feeling for what is just, but what is beautiful and what is true is to the same degree the object of his passion. He finds in each of these ideas the echoes of the other two, and completes, tempers, and broadens each one through the others. Phidias is in Pythagoras, and Socrates is in Phidias.

The Jews were bound to misunderstand Christ because he reacted as an artist against the ideal of justice which had made them unjust, and taught the lowly to pity the strong. The Greeks were far better prepared to understand Him. They knew Him from long ago. He was Dionysus, come from India and returning through Asia with the armies of Alexander; Dionysus the god of periodic resurrections, the god of primitive superstitions, of magics and sorceries, as he had been, in the time of Æschylus, the god of pagan drunkenness; Dionysus, the eternal god of the multitudes and of women. He was the God-man of their myths also, the hero, Herakles, Prometheus. Before Christ the Stoics had taught the conquest of the inner freedom, which is the measure of the discipline which we can impose on ourselves. Before Christ Socrates had died for man. The humanity of Christ was the testament of the ancient world rather than the preface to the new.

First it brought the sword. St. Paul was to betray Jesus and whisper into the darkened intell'gence of the moaning world the revenge of the Jewish mind. The philosophers were to turn their backs on Him, but the suffering slaves and the women, of whom our

GRECO-EGYPTIAN ART. Portrait of young girl, on papyrus (*Archæological Museum, Florence*).

mind as well as our flesh is born, the women forever watching that the fire may burn on the hearth—the slaves and the women hearken to Him. Man creates the ideal, but he tires of it. When the ideal burns out in him it is woman who picks it up to let it sleep in her until another male voice comes to awaken it there. If art is feminized and softened in the mind of men, as all the works of this age testify, the will becomes virile and tense in the heart of women. And it is the latter development which kills the former.

Reason was dying alone, skeptical and disdainful. Sentiment was growing up alone, blind and groping. It was to conquer. It was the crowd and it was life.

The sentimental uprising of the weak ruins civilization. We are about to burn the books, smash the statues, gut the human temples, and lose our contact with the earth. What does it matter? We must accept these downfalls. It is they that are the condition of the morrow which makes reparation. On the western soil, plowed by Greece, the real thought of Christ is to be reborn in the speech of Prometheus, after more than a thousand years of darkness, furies, and misunderstanding. Perhaps it is this abyss that is contemplated by the old portraits of the last Egypt, with their faces of enigma and their shadowy eyes in which a light trembles.

DELPHI.

Chapter VII. INTIMATE GREECE

I

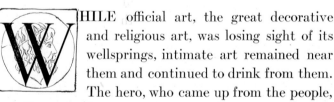HILE official art, the great decorative and religious art, was losing sight of its wellsprings, intimate art remained near them and continued to drink from them. The hero, who came up from the people, has disappeared, but the people is still there, and in it the Greek soul survives. The people undergoes the corrosive influence of intellectualism and of gold more slowly, and the flame of life smolders in it even when it is entirely extinguished on the upper levels. Even at the times of the worst decay the instinct of the multitudes contains all the elements of the higher life; only the awakening of new desires through the appearance of new needs is required to call forth the great

man and to ripen in him that instinct which the dead mass of his ancestors and the living mass of mankind have intrusted to him. Brutal animal power and the power of the intelligence are our only weapons for the conquest of our organization. The average civilized man, however, is as far from spiritual order as he is from direct possession. He has not yet attained the former; he has lost the latter. We are in the desert.

It is the people throughout the whole extent of the Greek world who gather up the scattered elements of the soul of antiquity. The workman of art takes the place of the hero. The uprooted tree is to cover the earth with leaves. From the pavement of the Greek cities emerges a world of trinkets, figurines of metal and of terra cotta, jewels, engraved stones, furniture, coins, and painted or incised vases. Yesterday the man of genius was at the service of the people. To-day the man of the people is at the service of the man of means.

The bond that unites the great artist with the artisan, the passage from the great sculpture to popular art, is the industry of terra-cotta figurines which were manufactured by thousands at Tanagra, among those Bœotian peoples whom the Athenians so greatly despised. The industry is not new. It had existed since Archaic times. But in the fourth century, influenced by the diffusion of taste, it was to perfect and extend itself. Like a little timid reflection it follows the evolution of the great focus. Archaic, when the latter is so, it becomes powerful and luminous with the focus; in the Praxitelean period the figurine

INTIMATE GREECE

is frankly intimate. But before Praxiteles, the reflection is totally lost in the blaze of the focus. From Praxiteles onward, when the focus is growing pale, the

Fragment of stele (end of VI Century).
(*Private Collection.*)

little reflection, on the contrary, becomes a shining point of light in the gathering shadow. The great sculpture which was made to decorate the temples and to live in space fails when it attempts to turn to to intimate things. The figurine, made to decorate private dwellings and to follow its owner to the tomb in order to win the gods over to him, is essentially intimate in inspiration and in destination. It was quite natural that it should attain its apogee in the century that brought the gods back among men. There are not many gods among the Bœotian sepulchers. There are men, and, above all, women and children, and even animals, toys, and obscene figures.

It has been said that Greek art lacked character. To assert this is to know it inadequately, and perhaps only by the calumnies which the academies, the Roman copies, and the retrospective novels have spread about it. What is character? It is the placing in evidence not of the picturesque, but of the descriptive elements of a given form. The art of the fifth century, which has been said not to have character, goes beyond individual character. It expresses the entire species, it describes it by insisting upon the dominant character of every individual. But the intimate art of Greece does not aim so high. With its charming wisdom it follows individual character.

TANAGRA.
Draped woman
(*Bibliotheque Nationale*).

People have forgotten the Greek portraits—so rare, it is true, but so penetrating—they have forgotten the Tanagras, the Myrinas, the vase paintings, the whole of Pompeiian painting, and those statuettes, those

TANAGRA. The toilet (*Private Collection*).

studies which perpetuate the cruel satire on the life of the sick, the hunchbacked, the lame, and the infirm of all kinds. They forget that there are even caricatures in the sepulchers of Tanagra. The popularity which the comedies of Aristophanes enjoyed is explained when we know their spectators. There was plenty of laughter in Greece, the philosophers laughed at the gods, the people laughed at the philosophers. The coroplasts (figure makers) of Tanagra and the potters of Ceramica were wholly joyous.

Pitcher (*National Museum, Athens*).

Did they imitate the great contemporary statues as often as has been said? It is improbable. There were occasional reminiscences, at the most. Imitation, close or loose, is death. Now these things live. All the qualities of Praxitelean sculpture are in them, and more acutely. They are modern. They will always be modern. It is because they are eternal. To make a living piece is to make something of eternity, to surprise the laws of life in their permanent dynamism.

Magna Græcia. Girls playing with osselets, terra cotta (*British Museum*).

Walking, dances, and games; the toilet, repose, gossip, attention, revery, immobility; the fine shadings of life, its impressions, and its memories—pass into these charming things, or flee, or hesitate, or halt. They are a living crowd of unseizable moments, these candid little creatures, with their red hair and their tinted dresses. They are the flowers that Greece gathers for a crown as she looks at herself in the water, runs under the willows, stands on tiptoe to reach the lips of the gods, and lives an animal life so ingenuous that her singers and her sculptors could not help deifying it and succeeding—as they followed its direction, without revolt and without a too laborious effort—in illumining its spirit.

These gracious creatures did not know their power of fascination. Greece loved and let herself be loved in an admirable innocence. If the grandiose sensualism of the Orient created the musical drama and inundated the sculptor of Olympia with its sacred frenzy, it did no more than graze the masses of the people and the artist-workmen who interpreted their needs. It is this that always separated Dorian and even Attic art, at least, in their average manifestations, from the art of the Greeks of the Orient. The women of Myrina, the Tanagra of Asia Minor, knew their power of love. The true soul of Asiatic Greece, ardent to the point of voluptuousness, the soul whose flame streams into the Hellenic intelligence, is in the art of Myrina, far more than in the decorative sculpture of the time. The richness of language is less disturbing in it than in the hands of the artist of Pergamos, for this little art—colorful, ardent, and impulsive—is made to be seen close by. There is not the least emphasis in this art; it is rich, almost brutal, a thing made to communicate the ardor of these beautiful, alluring women with their plump backs, their round arms, their heavy hair, their trailing dresses. They paint their questionable faces and adorn themselves and load

INTIMATE GREECE

themselves with jewels. One thinks of Hindoo sculpture which is soon to be stirring in the shadow of the caverns, of the idols of Byzantium with the gems glittering around them; one thinks of the splendid death, in the purple of Venice, of Oriental paganism. The conquest of the Occident by the woman of Asia is on the point of completion.

II

Everywhere, between the fourth and the first century — in Italy, in Sicily, on the shores of Asia Minor—the popular and intimate art causes official art to recede. The coroplast of Myrina and of Tanagra, and the sculptor of Alexandria remains himself, whereas the decorator of the monuments tries to catch once more a soul that has gone from him—that has gone out of the world—and to reconcentrate, by artificial means, the dissociated

TANAGRA (IV Century).
(*Museum of Chantilly.*)

elements of artistic creation. At Alexandria the figurine sculptor was doubtless not a workman, as at Myrina or at Tanagra, but rather one of those very brilliant, very superficial, and very skillful, fashionable artists who swarm around the rich man. Every new social expression, it is true, calls forth an art which adapts itself to it, which is beautiful simply because of that fact. But plutocratic societies constitute only a moment of that expression, the last before the downfall. It has been said that luxury called forth the arts. We may agree. But luxury consumes art, the profound creative feeling that comes out of the people in their full efforts, as the child from the mother's womb, the feeling that has in it their will, their hope, their power of illuminating. Between the statuette of the collector and the temples of a democracy there is the distance from the shelves of the drawing-room to the Acropolis.

During the Alexandrian period and even more during the imperial period, the diffusion of taste crowded out creative force. When this force manifests itself it often passes for an insult to taste or, at least, to the practical and moderate idea which the ruling classes and the world of fashion conceive of the mystic function of the artist; they imagine him made to satisfy their needs. To be sure, the taste of Alexandria is delightful—at least, the taste of the intellectual aristocracy; for the parvenu, there, as in other places, cares only for anecdotal art. Alexandria loves a whispering, tremulous, suave note in its production. Delicate little bronzes are created in which the material

TANAGRA. (IV Century). (*Private Collection.*)

takes on qualities of living flesh, of warm skin; it seems to cower from the cold like the virgin bodies so obligingly described by the sensual artist, in effete epochs, for the delight of the eye and the hand of the cultivated collector. Woman no longer unveils herself, the robes are stripped from her. Aphrodite no longer emerges from the sea; she enters the bathtub. She tries the water with her toes, her young body stoops or turns or stretches itself with a perfect absence of shame, and yet remains chaste, if one thinks of Asia, which attempts a last violent effort. Doubtless also, there is a debt to Egyptian purity, which Grecian nobility recognizes and weds.

Here is the fashionable drawing-room, here are rare pieces of furniture and the glass cases in which sleep precious things, sheltered from profaning hands. Polygraphy and romance have succeeded tragedy and history. It is the period when persons of elegance, men or women, covered from head to foot with amulets and jewels, eat and drink from chiseled metal. The locust, wrought of gold and worn in the hair, no longer sufficed for ladies of fashion. They needed rings, cameos, intaglios, necklaces, bracelets, clasps, and eardrops. The jewels of gold were, in Greece at least, of simple form, for Asia and imperial Rome have more pompous taste. The metal has the suppleness of a trailing vine, it creeps like a reptile over the forms, it weds the warm creases of the neck, it encircles the splendor of the arms, it draws the eye to the beautiful hands, it marries the dull sheen of the painted skin to its own tawny pallor. Set in a bezel or suspended, finely engraved stones bear images of the gods and portraits, birds, lions, beetles, and chimeras; there are as many amulets as there are superstitions in the epochs without faith.

Sicilian coins (*Bibliotheque Nationale*).

The cult of the stone for its own sake, for its arresting of light, was unknown to ancient art. The material must be wrought, must have imprinted in it man's idea of the universe, of himself, and of his destiny. In stone, in marble, bronze, gold, silver, ivory, wax, wood, and clay, in all the crystallizations of the earth, its bones, its flesh, its blood and its tears, the Greek of every land carved the form of his spirit. Some men have doubted the beauty of the chryselephantine sculpture of the fifth century as they have doubted the splendor which the temples of blue and gold must have taken on as they arose, under the immense Greek sky, from the forests and laurels of the acropolises and the promontories, giving to the white marble an indescribable quality of obsolute spirituality. When they carved Athena and Zeus in ivory or gold, the Greeks wanted only to express their veneration for them. But a mind like that of Phidias could not be mistaken in the medium. Behind his brow reigned order, lyric force, and the harmonious accord between intelligence and the heart, and if he carved gods in gold and ivory it was because gold and ivory obeyed him as marble did. What difference does the material make? Whatever it is, it expresses the artist as, in the crust of the earth, coal, and the diamond mingle and express its subterranean fire. The material is poured boiling into the mold of his soul; when his soul is strong, clay is strong as bronze, and when his soul is gentle, bronze is as tender as clay.

What good stuff the world is made of! Like the skin and the wool of the beasts, like the meat of the fruits, like bread, this stuff is man's companion. It is the water and the salt. It has the docility of the domestic creatures, it welcomes the master at his threshold and at his doorstep, protects him in the walls and the roofs, offers itself for his repose, hollows itself to receive his food, reaches up to lift its fruits to his lips and strives ingeniously to yield him materials less hard than itself. There was a time, toward the end of Hellenism, when wrought material surrounded man on every hand, like a motionless procession, at once defending and exalting him. Heroic art was weakening, doubtless, but the gods of ivory and gold were intact, deep in the sanctuaries, and the

INTIMATE GREECE 243

bright-painted marble heroes still inhabited the metopes where the gold of their bucklers glistened. Painted temples were everywhere, and propylæa, porticos, stadiums built of steps, colonnades, and terminal gods. The pavements of the streets were of marble, as were

TANAGRA (IV Century). (*Private Collection.*)

the steps of the acropolises and the serene amphitheaters looking over the hills to the sea. Gold and stone, jasper, agates, amethyst, cornelian, chalcedony, and rock-crystal went into the jewels which weighed on the arms, clasped the tunics, and shone in the dyed hair. And in the houses of marble, stone, or wood, and even in the depths of the sepulchers, were seats of marble or of wood, vases of gold, of silver, of bronze, statuettes of terra cotta or of metal, pots of clay or cups of onyx.

The hollow of the hand lent its warmth to precious bits of material, the piece of gold, silver, or copper. Greece did not invent the coin, it is true, but its cities were the first to give it its circular form, to place a head on one side, a symbol on the other, and an inscription composed of watchwords, signatures, or the value. With the diffusion of wealth and æsthetic culture, the coin springs from the bronze matrices in swarms. It is made practically everywhere, in Athens, Asia, Alexandria, and in Sicily especially, in the workshops of Syracuse. Coins mount from the Hellenic hearth like a shower of sparks. The type changes with the city, the events, the victories, and the traditions. Statues, celebrated pictures, legends, myths, symbolic animals, and incisive portraits, the reliefs polished by millions of hands and shaded with black in the hollows have the look of a living material made motionless by the mint. The circle is never a perfect one, the thickness of the disk varies; there, as in other cases, the equilibrium of the elements makes of the art object a complete organism, which symmetry would kill. The metal seems forced out from within as if swelling with juice and with a soul. The Greeks give to it a life of flesh or of the plant. On silver or gold vases they carve networks of twining branches, among which seeds, buds, and leaves—of the oak, the olive tree, the laurel, the plane tree or ivy—seem to tremble. Heavy fruit buries itself in the mystery of the foliage.

It is perhaps by these vases and by many of the terra cotta figurines that we can best judge to what degree the Greeks understood the frame in which the human figure moves. The setting was not a dominant idea with them as it was later on with the Hindoos and the men of the Renaissance—especially the Flemings and the Frenchmen of the Renaissance—because the soil of Greece was less rich in animate forms and because the Greeks looked on man as the ripe fruit; it

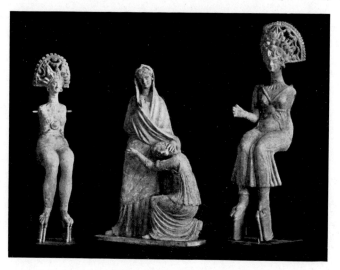

Myrina. Statuettes, terra cotta (*Louvre*).

was the fruit that constantly attracted them, whereas the branches, the trunk, and the ground in which the tree grew seemed to them only accompaniments to the superior melody realized by the mind. But their great tragic poets saw the mænads, dressed in tiger skins and girdled with serpents, crowned with flowers and leafy vine branches, bounding out of the forests with the panthers; they spoke of those monstrous unions from which the beast-man came, to affirm the grand accord of indifferent nature and the mind guided by will. And the humblest of their peasants, who knew that the spring and the grotto were peopled with familiar divinities, was at peace as he felt the fraternity of his soil.

III

The Greeks introduced into their house the world of the air and the plants. The cadaver of Pompeii, a city of Magna Græcia, built and decorated by Greeks, is covered with flowers. In the inner rooms, in the markets, everywhere are garlands of flowers, fruits, and leaves; there are birds and fishes, dense, shining, fiery still-life pieces surrounding false windows and painted floors which open on perspectives of streets and squares, of architecture and streets. It is doubtless only a translated, Latinized Greece, different from classic Greece and much affected by influences of Alexandria, of Asia, and inspired above all by the sea-sky, the vegetation, the red rocks, the flame, and the wine mulled on hot coals. Theocritus was a Syracusan, it is true. But on the soil of Greece there are bas-reliefs, vase-sculptures, Tanagra groups—satyrs, nymphs, young women, dancers, divinities of the woods and torrents—around whom we hear the purling of water, the rustle of leaves, the lowing and sharp bleating of the beasts, and flutes laughing and crying in the wind. And if surrounding nature stilled her voices for a moment to let Phidias commune with himself as he wrote into the human form alone his understanding of the world, Sophocles went to sit in the grove of Colonna, the grove of orange trees with its many crickets where the brooks ripple under the moss; Pindar, the rugged poet of the north, while journeying to the games by routes which took him to gorges and beaches, picked up on his way some formidable images, full of the sky and the ocean; Æschylus, from the top of the Acropolis of Argos, watched the night sparkle, and from the most distant past of Hellas a cool breeze was blown. Ægean art is already alive with forms of the sea. The sea wind, the water of the river, and the murmur of the foliage are witnesses to the meeting of Ulysses and Nausicaa, whom the hero compares to the stem of a palm tree. Does not Vitruvius affirm that the Doric comes from the male torso, the Ionic from the female torso?

Syrian statuette
(*From Le Musee*).

In any case, this rather limited Pompeiian art, made up, as it is, of recollections and distant imitations, and due almost entirely to the brush of hired decorators and of house painters, breathes the animal and the material world, the swarming and confused world that surrounds us. How young it still is, despite the old age of the pagan civilizations; how vigorous it is with all its vague mossiness; how profound and full of the antique soul! What persuasion there is in its power, and, on the monochrome backgrounds—red, black, green, or blue—how broad and spontaneous the stroke is, how sure, how intense in expression, and how living the form! Amors, dancers, winged geniuses, gods or goddesses, animals, forms nude, draped, or aureoled with wavy gauzes, legends, battles, and all the ancient symbolism so near the soil live again here, with a slightly gross sensualism and with the candor of the workmen who interpret, certainly, but with that calm, that almost unspoiled freshness, that virginity of life which were known only to the ancient world. The dancing forms appear half veiled, with their pure arms and pure legs continuing the pure torso, like balanced branches. The nude bodies emerge gently from the shadow, floating in their firm equilibrium. Here and there are implacable portraits with large, ardent eyes—with life in its brutal austerity, undiminished by any visible intermediary. At times, side by side with the Greek soul, and bearing a germ of academism that, fortunately, is still unconscious, there is that ardent expressiveness which, thirteen centuries later, was to characterize the awakening of Italy. It is to be seen in that "Theseus Victorious over the Minotaur," which the great Masaccio would have loved. It is an anxious, uneven world, with currents of influence running through it in every direction, but fiery and brilliant, rotten at the top, and yet ingenuous underneath.

See in these portraits the sense of immensity that is in the gaze, how the great figures are steeped in

INTIMATE GREECE 249

thought, and how a tremor seems to run inward through their living immobility. This arrested life is almost terrible to look upon. One would say that it had

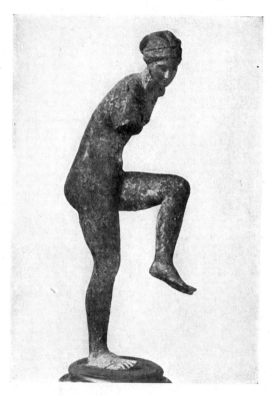

HELLENISTIC ART. Aphrodite, bronze statuette (*British Museum*).

been suddenly fixed, as if seized by the volcano at the same hour as the city was. Impressionism, do you say? Yes, in its fire, in its breadth, in the way in which the movement is instantaneously surprised; but however much weakened, however enervated the voice of the artisans of a corrupt and skeptical age, this painting expresses a power of comprehension and a depth of love that only a few isolated men attain to-day. It is the only real renascence of Greek heroism. It responds, like the "Hercules of the Belvedere" and the Venuses of the valley of the Rhone, to the shock of Hellenic intelligence as it meets with Latin force and, in a flash, creates an art complete in its vigor, its ardent life, and its feverish concentration.

Although these paintings are not, properly speaking, copies (if we admit that a copy is possible and that the copyist, whether mediocre or touched with genius, does not in every case substitute his nature for that of the master), although they are only reminiscences, the transplantation of Greek works on a renewed soil, it is through them that we can get an idea—even if a distant one—of the painting of antiquity, which the crumbling of the temples has wiped out. The most celebrated frescoes of the dead city recalled the works of Polygnotus, Zeuxis, Parrhasios, and Apelles. The painting related the ancient myths and the story of the national wars. At first it knew flat colors only, very much simplified, doubtless, very brilliant and hard tones, brutal in their oppositions, before modeling appeared with Parrhasios. The lines which inclosed the powerful polychromy must have had the firmness of the uninterrupted curve which the passage of the hills to the plains and of bays to the sea taught to the men who were at this time making the gods. Always decorative in its beginnings, it undergoes the fate of the painting of modern schools, where the easel picture appears when the statues descend from their heights on the temples to invade the public squares, apartments, and gardens. Like sculpture, this painting had to bend to the will of the rich man. But doubt-

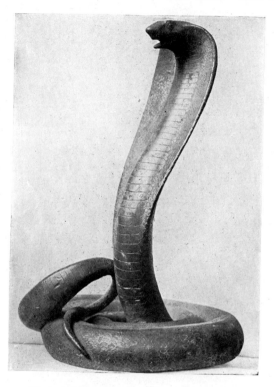

Uræus, bronze (*Bibliotheque Nationale*).

less it retained its character better, being more supple, more a thing of shades, more individualistic, more the master of saying only what it did not want to hide. I see it, after Parrhasios, as somewhat like Venetian painting around Giorgione and Titian: ripe, warm, autumnal, with an evanescent modeling in the colorful shadows and dazzling in the parts which stand out and which seem turned to gold by the sap from within. It is less fluid and musical, however—more massive, more compact. Oil painting has not been discovered, and the wax renders the work slower and less immaterial.

IV

In any case it has preserved until our time, through Pompeii, the perfume of the Greek soul, of which it hands on to us one of the most mysterious aspects, far better than does the art of ceramics, which has traced that soul for us in hardly anything more than its external evolution—in such matters as composition, superficial technique, and subjects. The role of ceramics is limited, with the little terra cottas, to representing the national industrial art of Greece—which is already saying a good deal. But it cannot pretend to stand for more than the reflection in the popular soul of the flowers gathered by certain minds throughout the nation.

Hundreds of workshops had been opened practically everywhere, in Athens, in Sicily, in Etruria, in Cyrenaica, in the Islands, in the Euxine, in a place as distant, even, as the Crimea. The most celebrated painters of cups, Euphronius, Brygos, and Douris, worked with their workmen, often repeated themselves, copied one another and rivaled one another in activity so as to attract patrons. Through the goodly communion of their work, through their continual exchange and emulation, they founded a pow-

Pompeii (I Century A.D.). Telephus suckled by a doe, fresco (*Naples Museum*).

erful industry. In it, as in other activities, except where Greece was dominated by Sparta, the slave collaborated with the master, whether as a farmer in the country, as a servant in the city or as an artisan in the workshop; he was, beyond all doubt, less unhappy than the feudal serfs or the wage-earner of to-day. Man was too wise, at that time, to utilize the sufferings of man for his profit; life was too simple, too near the soil, too merged with the light to take the law of hell as its model.

Industrial art, however, in spite of these powerful roots, is so limited by its very purposes, that it cannot pretend to such high intention as that of the art which governs the sculpture of the gods. On the other hand, it avoids, for a much longer time, the double snare of pretentiousness and of fashion. Thus it dies less quickly and renews itself more readily. Diderot was right in re-establishing the dignity of the industrial arts. He was wrong in placing them on the same level with the others. The sculptor, and more especially the painter, in his struggle with the material, is guided only by the quality of the material. The purpose of the object allows it to move in so wide an area that the liberty of these artists knows no other limits than those of the infinite space in which occur the relationships of intelligence and sensibility with the whole universe of sensations and images. The artisan is confined between narrower frontiers by the function of the furniture or the ornament on which he works, and also by its size. A fresco and a thimble do not offer identical means to their creators. If the

INTIMATE GREECE

murmur of the soul can be as pure, as touching, in one as in the other, the elements of the symphony are far less numerous in the latter case, and infinitely less

POMPEII (I Century A.D.). Theseus, conqueror of the Minotaur, fresco (*Naples Museum*).

complex. And, before practical utility, spiritual utility is obliged to retreat.

In addition, the workman must arrange, in such a way, the ornaments with which he wants to decorate the object, so that they will follow the contour of its forms, to modify themselves according to its volume and its surfaces, and, like himself, accept a role which excludes all others and which is, even so, of an inferior

HERCULANEUM. Faun playing on pipes, fresco
(*Naples Museum*).

order. And thus it is that only in very rare cases do we discover on the sides of even the most beautiful Athenian vases a hint of that logical composition which places the great sculpture on the plane of the universal. Forms elongate and become parallel to wed the flanks of the amphoras, to make them straight and to give them spring. They stretch in encircling

INTIMATE GREECE

rings around the cups, the vases, and the bowls as if to drag the pot along in a spinning movement. Here and there, undoubtedly very often, in an ensemble at once fiery and sober, easily read at a glance, black on red or red on black, there are admirable details, draw-

Cantharus of Epigenes (*Louvre*).

ing as pure as the line of the landscape, incisive as the mind of the race, and suggesting the absent modeling by its direction alone and its manner of indicating attitude and movement. For the workman as for the sculptor of the temple, the mold of the Archaic is broken, nature is no longer a world of immutable and separate forms, but a moving world, constantly combining and disuniting itself, renewing its aspects and changing the elements of its relationships at every second.

The form of these vases is so pure that one would

say it had been born unaided, that it had not come from the hands of the potters, but from the obscure and permanent play of the forces of nature. We have a vague sensation before these vases, as if the artist

Votive helmet, bronze (*Louvre*).

were obeying the hints of the wheel as he presses in or swells out the clay, thickens the paste or spreads it. When the wheel hums, when the material whirls and flies, an inner music murmurs to the moving form the mysterious fluctuation which gives songs and dances

INTIMATE GREECE

their rhythm. Grain, breasts, round haunches, closed flowers, open flowers, twining roots, spherical forms of nature—the central mystery of them all sleeps in the still hollow of the vases. The law of universal attraction does not control the suns alone, but all matter moves and turns in the same circle. Man tries to escape from the rhythm, and rhythm always draws

Cup of Chelis (*Louvre*).

him back again. The vase has the form of fruits, of the mother's belly, and of the plants. The sphere is the matrix and the tomb of forms. Everything comes out of it. Everything returns to it.

Save in the case of the great Panathenaic amphoras which have the severity of design proper to their use, the Greek vase almost always welcomes you with a charming sense of the intimate. When it recounts the adventures of war or interprets the old myths, it humanizes itself delightfully. Very often there are children at their games, men in their workshop, women at their toilet, long, undulating, and rich forms indicated with a continuous line. The familiar painting of the Egyptian husbandman told of the work of the fields. The familiar painting of the Greeks, a people of traders and talkers, speaks rather of household work.

The legend of the stern heroism of every-day existence is no more born out by these vases than by the

MAGNA GRÆCIA. Olive vase, silver, Treasury of Boscoreale (*Louvre*).

Bœotian figurines. Life in the ancient city tends toward a kindly, sometimes difficult, equilibrium. The passages between its component elements are more noticeable in speech and in the written law than in reality. Southern indulgence and familiarity draw everything together. If the Greek had looked down on woman he would not have spoken of her with so much intelligent love, and if he had been harsh toward his servitor he would not have shown him thus associated with his own tasks. The child plays and goes to school, where he learns music, writing, and recitation. The ephebus frequents the stadium, the men, young and old, frequent the agora, the housewife spins and sews. On feast days, the young girls, like bending reeds, like undulating water, like waving flowers and garlands, dance in long lines, making rhythmical—to the sound of the shrill music—the movements of the march, of the pursuit, of the farewell, of supplication, of prayer, of a voluptuousness unconscious of itself —a full epitome of the essential moments of our life. Passion? The Greek knew it so well that he deified it, but it was for him a food, the passage from one state of equilibrium to another; he had the intuitive feeling that the impulse of sentiment was only a means of realizing harmony.

Funerary stele (v Century B.C.). (*National Museum, Athens.*)

Ares and Aphrodite had their temples, Dionysus also, but outside of Eleusis—a veiled summit, a mysterious region where, doubtless, the unity of our desire was revealed—the three summits of Greece were the Parthenon of Athens, the sanctuary of Delphi, and the Altis of Olympia, where man came to adore Reason, Beauty, and Energy. Heroism is life accepted.

It is the progressive and never-attained realization of the conquests that life imposes on us.

Submission to destiny—therein is Greece. There are in Athens, in the little cemetery of Ceramica at the foot of the Acropolis, certain funeral steles of a moving symbolism. Greece so wanted us to love life that she expressed her desire even on the stone of the tomb. Farewells are said there with simple gestures, with slightly sad and perfectly calm faces, as if the persons were going to see each other again. Friend clasps the hand of friend, the mother touches the child's hair with her fingers, the serving maid hands to the mistress her jewel casket. The familiar animals come, to be present at the departure. The glory of terrestial life enters the subterranean shadow.

THE ROMAN CAMPAGNA.

Chapter VIII. ROME

I

NTIL the Hellenistic period the radiance of Greece in the Mediterranean world prevented men from perceiving the civilizations which were growing up or disappearing round about her. The nation she knew best and of which she spoke most favorably was Persia, because it was the power she had to combat. The old peoples had hardly more than one means of intermingling with and comprehending one another, which was war. Now, military conquest was repugnant to the Greeks. The colonies which they had sown on all the shores of Asia, the Euxine, North Africa, southern Italy, and Sicily constituted a network of stations in their vast maritime system which was pretty closely reserved for the nation, and beyond which everything, for them, was legends, semidarkness, and confusion. Trade scarcely got beyond the coasts of the happy seas. The interior of the lands, the mountains of the horizon, the unknown forests, with-

ETRUSCAN ART (VI Century B.C.). Sarcophagus, detail (*Villa of Pope Julius*).

held their secret from Greece, since they escaped her influence.

Hellenism has left only furtive traces outside of the Greek world, properly so-called. There was, perhaps, only one agricultural and nonmaritime people that was strongly influenced by Greece, through the cities of Magna Græcia and through the sea routes. The country that lies between the Arno, the Tiber, the

Apennines, and the sea was probably the only one of the old world to accept, without resistance, and from the heroic period onward, the supremacy of the Greek spirit. The Etruscans, like the Greeks, were doubtless descended from the old Pelasgians, and recognized in the products brought them by the ships—vases especially, which they bought in large quantities— the encouragement of an effort related to their own. In fact the most original manifestations of their art always owe something to Greece and, certainly by intermediation of the latter, to Assyria and to Egypt.

In time, undoubtedly, if Rome had not come to crush the germ of Etruscan genius, the latter would have profited by the decline of Greece, for the realization of itself through contact with its soil. It is a rugged land of torrents, forests, and mountains, well drawn and well defined. But the Etruscan peasant, bent over his furrow, in his landscape where the eye is constantly arrested by the hills, did not have the free horizon that opened before the man of Greece trafficking among the bays and islands, or tending his sheep on the heights. Hence, there is in Etruscan art something funereal, violent, and bitter.

The priest reigns. Forms are inclosed in tombs. In the sculpture of the sarcophagi we frequently find two strange figures leaning on their elbows with the stiffness and the mechanical expression known to all archaisms—the lower part of their bodies unconnected with the secret and smiling upper part; the frescos of the funerary chambers tell a tale of sacrifices and killings; the whole art is fanatical, superstitious, and agitated. The myth and the technique often come from the Greeks. But we seem to have something here which resembles more the hell which the Pisan primitives are to paint, twenty centuries later, on the walls of the Campo Santo, than it does the harmonies

ETRUSCAN ART. Tomb of the Augurs, fresco, detail (*Corneto Tarquinia*).

of Zeuxis. Tuscan genius is already piercing through, underneath these bizarre, over-elongated, and somewhat sickly forms, wherein the vigor and elegance of the race fail to overcome the enervated mysticism. None the less a strange force, a mysterious life wells up in them. These somber frescos look like the shadows which one might trace on a wall. An all-powerful decorative genius reveals itself in them, an equilibrium constantly pursued and given style to by the visible symmetry of the ritual gestures, of the flight of birds, of the branches, the leaves, and the flowers. It seems a kind of dance, caught in the instant of its most fleeting rhythm.

Etruria, as the educator of Rome, was the intermediary step of civilization on its march from the

ETRUSCAN ART. Cinerary urn (*Perugia*).

East to the West. The material remains of the Roman Republic teach us, perhaps, more about the genius of the Etruscans than about that of the founders of the city. The vault, which the Pelasgians brought from Asia, and which their Ægean descendants gave to primitive Greece, is transmitted to Rome by their Italic descendants in Italy. The Roman arch of triumph is only a modified Etruscan gate. Rome had the "Cloaca Maxima" built by architects from Etruria, and it forms the intestines of the city, the vital organ around which its profound materialism is to install itself, to grow little by little and extend its arms of stone over the whole of the ancient world. The Etruscan, from the sixth century onward, not only brings to Rome his religion and his science of augury, he digs the sewers, builds the temples, erects the first statues; he forges the arms by which Rome is to reduce him to subjection. He casts bronze, and his bronzes, in which he reveals his genius for uncompromising expression, have a bitter force that is as rugged and hard as the oak clumps of the Apennines. The symbol of Rome, the rough she-wolf of the Capitol, was made by an old Tuscan bronze worker.

II

From her beginnings Rome is herself. She diverts to her profit the moral sources of the old world as she diverts the waters of the mountains to bring them inside her walls. The source once captured, her avidity exhausts it, and she goes on farther to capture another. At the beginning of the third century Etruria has been crushed by Rome, and her blood and nerves have been mingled with those of the Latins and the Sabines. And this is the cement which holds together the block on which Rome is to support herself, to spread over the world the concentric circles of her vital effort. All the resistance she encounters,

ETRUSCAN ART. Fresco (*Corneto Tarquinia*).

Pyrrhus, Carthage, and Hannibal, will be to her only so many instruments for cultivating her will and for increasing it. The legions progress like the regular deposit of a river.

If Roman positivism had not pressed the Latin and Etruscan together, one asks, as one reads Plautus, Lucretius, Vergil, and Juvenal, what art could have realized this rough synthesis of the Italic peoples, with their love of woods and gardens, their genius, as bitter as the leaves of their trees, and as rich as their plow-lands? But the Roman was bent too much on external conquests to conquer all his own vigor and harshness. As long as war continued methodically —five or six centuries—he had not the time to express himself. As soon as the springs relaxed, the mind of conquered Greece upset the whole mechanism. Mummius, after the sack of Corinth, said to the contractors charged with getting the spoil to Rome: "I warn you that if you break those statues you will have to make new ones to replace them."

Such a misunderstanding of the higher role of the work of art has about it something sacred. A candor is revealed therein from which a people may expect everything, if it is also the characteristic of that people's viewing of life. For Rome it would have been salvation, if she had refused the masterpieces which the Consul sent to her. But she accepted them eagerly, she had others sent, and still others; she devastated Greece, and her hard spirit wore itself down on that diamond.

We have, in this, one of the fatalities of history, and

the proof of the tendency in the ensemble of human societies to seek its equilibrium. Subjected materially, a people of superior culture morally subjects the people that conquered it. Chaldea imposed its mind on

Etruscan Art.   She-wolf (*Museum of the Capitol*).

Assyria, Assyria and Ionian Greece did the same with Persia, Greece transforms the Dorian. Rome wants to please Greece as the parvenu does the aristocrat, Greece wants to please Rome as the weak does the strong. In this contact Greece can no longer prostitute a genius which had long since escaped from her; but Rome loses part of her own genius.

The Roman, in his manners, his temperament, his religion, his whole moral substance, differed totally from the Greek. In the case of the latter we have a simple, free, investigating life, given over completely to realizing the inner harmony which a charming imagination pursues along every path. In the case of the Roman, life is disciplined, egoistic, hard, and firm; it seeks its nutriment outside of itself. The

Bust of Tiberius, bronze
(*National Museum, Rome*).

Greek makes the city in the image of the world. The Roman wants to make the world in the image of the city. The true religion of the Roman is the hearth, and the chief of the hearth is the father. The official cult is purely decorative. The divinities are concrete

Claudius (I Century A.D.). (*Louvre.*)

things, fixed, positive, without connection, without harmonious envelope, one personified fact beside another personified fact. They belong to a domain apart and, in reality, quite secondary. On one side divine right and religion, on the other human right and jurisprudence. It is the contrary of Greece where the passage is an insensible one from man to god, from the real to the possible. The Greek ideal is diversity and continuity in the vast harmonic ensemble of actions and reactions. The Roman ideal is the artificial union of these isolated elements in a stiff and hard ensemble. If the art of this people is not utilitarian, it is certain to be conventional.

Why should Rome take the elements of these formal conventions from others than Greece, who offered them to her? There are to be, indeed, attempts at transformation, and even her instinct is to rebel confusedly. In spite of itself, against itself, a people is itself. The Greek temple cannot be transported to Rome, like the statues and the paintings, and when the Roman architect returns from Athens, from Sicily, or from Pæstum, he has had the time on his journey unconsciously to transform the science he has brought back from those places. The column becomes thick and smooth, often useless, placed against the wall in the guise of an ornament. If the Corinthian order dominates, the Doric and Ionic transformed, make frequent appearances, often mingling or superposing themselves in the same monument. The temple, almost always larger than in Greece, loses its animation. It is voluntarily symmetrical, massive, heavy, positive.

Outside of Rome—in Gaul, in Greece, in Asia especially, Rome constructs formidable temples, resplendent with force and sunlight, on which the high plant growth

GRECO-ROMAN ART. Wrestler, bronze
(*Louvre*).

of the Corinthian looks like living trees cemented into the wall. But buildings like these are rare on Italian soil. In them, doubtless, Rome only played her habitual part of severe administrator. The temples of Hellenic Gaul are Greek, the temples of Asia have the sumptuousness and the redoubtable grandeur of everything that rises above this mystic, feverish soil, saturated with rottenness and heat, and for which time does not count. Everywhere, for the utilitarian monuments even—for the arenas of Provence (to cite no more than these) present themselves with a discretion, a grace, an unstudied elegance which one does not find in those of Italy—everywhere the native soil imposes on Rome its collaboration and, sometimes, its domination. In ornament, for example, we find among the Greeks, the Asiatics, the Africans, or the Spaniards working under the Roman constructor, the silent insurrection of personal sentiment. Certain Gallo-Roman bas-reliefs, by their savor and their verve, by the blithe vigor with which the stone is attacked, by the concrete and perhaps slightly bantering tenderness of their accent, immediately make one think of the leaves, the fruits, the garlands, and the figures which, ten centuries later, are to adorn the capitals, the porches, and the façades of the French cathedrals. It is only in the general ordonnance of the edifice that the Roman retains his rights.

The Greeks variegated their monuments with ocher and vermilion, blue, green, and gold; the building shone in the light. How should the Roman understand polychromy? Painting has something mobile and fugitive about it, something almost aerial, which is repellent to his genius. He sees it already paling and wearing off from the marbles of the Acropolis. Therefore, he incorporates it in the material, he makes a temple wherein multicolored marbles, simple or veined, alternate with granites, porphyries, and basalts.

GRECO-ROMAN ART. Bacchante, fresco
(*Museum of the Vatican*).

Harmony scarcely counts; the color is to change no more.

III

The same transformation everywhere—in painting, in sculpture. The copy, even when conscientious, is

Tomb of Cecilia Metella (I Century B.C.).

always unfaithful. It is made heavy, pasty, and laborious; it is dead. The Greek statue maker, working in Rome, sometimes has beautiful awakenings, but he obeys the fashion—now he is classical, now decadent, now archaistic. As to the Roman statue maker, his work is to manufacture for the collector innumerable replicas of the statues of the great period of Athens. It is the second step in that academism from which the modern world is still suffering. The first dated from those pupils of Polycleitus, of Myron,

The Pont du Gard (19 B.C.).

of Phidias, and of Praxiteles who knew their trade too well.

Rome encumbers itself with statues. There are the dead and the living. All those who have held public office, high or low, want to have under their eyes the material and durable witness of the fact. Far more, each one, if he can pay for it, wants to know in advance the effect that will be produced by the trough of marble in which he is to be laid away. It is not only the Imperator who is to see his military life made illustrious in the marble of the triumphal arches and columns. The centurion and the tribune surely have, in their public life, some high deed to hand down for the admiration of the future. The sculptors of the sarcophagi devise the anecdotal bas-relief. Historical "genre," that special form of artistic degeneration, which at all times has so comfortably kept house with

ROME (I Century A.D.). The Colosseum. Interior of the arena.

academism, is invented. The great aim is to find and relate as many heroic deeds as possible in the life of the great man. On five or six meters of marble adventures are heaped up, personages, insignia, weapons, and fasces are squeezed in. Everything is episodic, and one seizes nothing of the episode; whereas in the sober Greek bas-relief where nothing was episodic, the whole signification of the scene appeared at a glance. And yet it is, above all, in these bas-reliefs that the harsh Roman genius has left its trace. There is very often a kind of somber force and a solemnity there which affect us sharply, carrying with them a train of crushing memories—the laurels, the lictors, the consular purple. In these bas-reliefs there bursts forth a barbarous power which no education can

ROME. Thermæ of Titus, central gallery.

restrain. Sometimes, even, in the heavy chiseled garlands where the fruits, the flowers, and the foliage accumulate and heap up like the harvests and vintages of the strong Latin Campagna, one feels the mounting of the rustic sap which Rome could not dry up and which swells in the poems of Lucretius as in an old tree that sends out green shoots again. Then the Greeks are forgotten, and the sculptors from Athens must laugh in pity before these confused poems to the riches of the earth. And doubtless they prefer the heavy imitations of themselves that are made. There are no more empty places, to be sure, no more silent passages, no longer any wave of uniting volumes that reply to one another in their constant need for musical equilibrium. But it is a disciplined orgy, even so, whose opulence is an element to be incorporated with the intoxication of the flesh rather than inscribed in the mind. The landscape background of the Roman, on the whole, affirms itself as less stylized, doubtless, but more moving and sensual than the Greek setting. One hears the crunch of the vintagers' feet on the grapes, the oak offers armfuls of firm acorns and black leaves, the ears of wheat loaded with grains group themselves into thick sheaves, we smell the floating perfume of green boughs and the odor of the plowed soil —and the richness and density of all this sculpture are due, probably, to workmen only. In the production of the official statue maker, on the contrary, a violent confusion reigns, monotonous ennui and immobility.

Such a spirit is entirely foreign to man, it is devoted entirely to glorifying beings, things, and abstractions toward which man is not drawn by his true nature, but by prejudice, or the cult of the moment. And it was to this spirit that allegory owed the favor which it enjoyed under Roman academism. The great artist does not love allegory. If it is imposed on him, he dominates it, he drowns it in form, drawing from form itself the sense that is always in it. Allegory, on the

POLA (I Century A.D.). The Arena, detail.

284   ANCIENT ART

other hand, dominates the false artist, to whom form says nothing. Allegory is the caricature of the symbol. The symbol is the living visage of the realized abstraction; allegory has to mark the presence of the abstraction by external attributes.

These cold academic studies, these mannikins of

Sarcophagus of Julius Bassus (*Vatican*).

bronze and of marble, these frozen gestures—always the same—these oratorical or martial attitudes which knew no change, these rolls of papyrus, these draperies, these tridents, lightnings, and horns of plenty crowded themselves, heavy and tiresome, into all the public places, into forums, squares, and sanctuaries. Sarcophagi and statues were made in advance; the orator dressed in his toga, the general in his cuirass, the tribune, the quæstor, the consul, the senator, **or** the imperator, could be supplied at any time. The body was interchangeable. The head was screwed on to

The wife of Trajan (*British Museum*).

the shoulders. To recognize the personage one had to look at the face, which would sometimes be placed too high to be distinguishable. It was the only thing that did not have the appearance of having come from the factory. It alone responded to a need for truth, an obscure and material need, but a sincere one. It was made only after the order had been given and from the person who ordered it; thereafter, the artist and the model collaborated honestly.

There is something implacable about all these Roman portraits. There is no convention, but also no fantasy. Man or woman, emperor or noble, the model is followed feature by feature, from the bone-structure of the face to the grain of the skin, from the form of the hair dressing to the irregularities of the noses and the brutality of the mouths. The marble cutter is attentive, diligent, and of complete probity. He does not think even of emphasizing the descriptive elements of the model's face, he wants to make it a *likeness*. There is not the least attempt at generalizing, no attempt at lies or flattery or satire—no concern with psychology and little character, in the descriptive sense of the word. There is less of penetration than of care for exactitude. If the artist does not lie, neither does the model. These are historical documents, from the real Cæsars of Rome to the adventurers of Spain or of Asia, from deified monsters to Stoic emperors. Where is the classic type of the "profile like a medal" in these heads? They may be heavy or delicate, square, sharp-featured, or round, at times dreamy, often wicked, but they are always true, whether puffed-up play actors, slightly foolish idealists, wholly incurable brutes, weather-beaten old centurions, or crowned hetairæ who are not even pretty. Some of these heads, certainly, through their

Segovia (ii Century A.D.). Aqueduct.

quality of attention, and the intensity with which life concentrates in them, by their density and mass, by the pitiless pursuit of the profound modeling which the bone structure of the interrogated face possesses by chance and reveals to the sculptor, are of a powerful beauty. In the statue of the Great Vestal, for example, immediate truth attains the stage of typical truth: then the whole of Rome, with its domination of itself, and the weight it laid on the world, appears in this strong and grave woman; it is as solid as the citadel, as safe as the hearth, without humanity, without tenderness, and without weakness, until the day when slowly, deeply, irresistibly, it is to have plowed its furrow.

IV

We must turn our back on the temples, give scarcely a glance to the massive arches and columns of triumph. Around them the brutal mounting of the processions lifts the power of Rome to an empyrean no higher than their summit. The Rome, which wanted to be and believed itself to be an artist, put the whole of its native genius into the marble portraits and into certain bas-reliefs of startling authority and ruggedness. To find this genius again in more characteristic and disproportionately imposing manifestations, we must leave the domain of art, properly so-called, of that superior function whose role is to exalt all the higher activities of the intelligence and of love. We must consider the expressions of Rome's positive and materialistic daily life. Rome had no other moral need

ROME

than that of proclaiming her external glory, and any monument sufficed for that, provided it was graced with the name of temple, arch of triumph, rostrum, or trophy. But Rome had great needs in matters of health, physical strength, and, later on—in order to pour out this health and strength which had grown

Temple of Jupiter at Baalbeck, detail (II Century A.D.).

too heavy to bear after the end of the wars—it had great need of food, of women, and of violent games. Hence the paved roads, the bridges, and aqueducts at first, and afterwards the theaters, the baths, and the circuses—blood and meat after travel and water.

The Roman ideal throughout history has the uniformity and the constancy of an administrative regulation. In Rome the real artist is the engineer, as the true poet is the historian and the true philosopher is the jurist. The Roman imposes on the family, on society, and on nature the form of his will. He represses his instinct for rapine; by living on himself he acquires the moral vigor necessary to conquer the earth; he escapes from his arid surroundings by reaching out with his tentacles of stone to the ends of the world. He plans the whole of his work—his law, his annals, and his roads, with one paving stone after the other, just as, starting from Rome, he extends over the plains, the mountains, and the sea, circle after circle of his domination.

The pride of this people and its strength were the sites where it dwelt—a few low hills amid the marshes, from which the inhabitants of the Sabine heights and the plowman of Latium flee. There is neither bread nor water, the view is closed by a distant circle of hostile mountains. It is a refuge of pariahs, but of violent and voracious pariahs who know that there are fat lands, rich cities, and herds behind the horizon. Cost what it may, they must break through the accursed circle. The race is to draw its strength from the mountain springs which rigid paths of stone are to spread in torrents over Rome. Rigid lines of stone are to direct that force across the dry marshes, across the open forests, the rivers, solitudes, and mountains, to the light of the south and the mists of the north. Cement binds the stones and the slabs of the pavement, making of them a single, continuous block, from the center of the inhabited world to its boundaries. Blood starts from the heart. Rome is in the whole empire, the whole empire is in Rome. The ancient world is an immense oasis of woods, of plowed lands, of opulent cities, and fecund oceans; Rome is a mass of walls and huts, a surge, black and low, of the dens of the people; its noise never ceases, it crowns itself

ORANGE (II Century A.D.). The Theater.

laboriously with hard buildings of stone, heavy in their form and in their silence. Between the world and the city lies a mournful desert crossed by rigid arteries; as far as the circle of the horizon, it is a sad tract of country, undulating like a sea under the sun or the night.

Thus to weld this isolated city to the rest of the world, materially and morally, an enormous pride was needed, an enormous energy, and enormous works that increased this energy, exalted this pride, and incited it to undertake works still more enormous. Under the Empire the tendency toward the enormous quickens till it becomes a wild pace. More aqueducts, bridges, and roads, more stones beside stones. With Asia subjected and peace imposed, the thirst for pleasure and the freedom needed for it made their entry into Rome. The city gives itself up to enjoyment with all the strength it had devoted to conquest and authority. The enormous is in demand more and more—in play, in love, in idleness, as in war, law, history, and the construction of the city. Rome is no longer content to make the pulsations of its heart felt to the limits of her empire, she is not to rest until she has brought the material of the empire back to herself. Men of all races congest her streets, bringing with them their manners, their gods, and their soil. "The climates are conquered, nature is subjected; the African giraffe and the Indian elephant walk about Rome under a movable forest; vessels fight on land."[1] After the aqueducts and the roads, amphitheaters are constructed, circuses in which armies kill each other, where eighty thousand Romans can see all the beasts of the desert, forest, and mountain let loose upon men, while pools of hot blood dampen the blood already clotted. Thermæ are built with tanks in which three thousand persons can bathe at ease, immense tepidariums, promenades with monstrous vaults, where the idler passes his day amid women, dancers, musicians, rhetoricians, sophists, and statues brought from Greece. But the soul of Greece did not enter with

[1] Michelet, *Histoire Romaine*.

them. The Greek, even to the days of his saddest decline, loved these forms for themselves. The Roman sees in them a fit frame for his orgy of the flesh, of blood, of streaming waters. He plunges with frenzy into his heavy sensuality.

But in that, at least, without knowing it, he is an

Arena of Nimes (II Century A.D.).

artist. The activity is of a low form, doubtless—quite positive, egoistic, cruel, and not to be freed from materialism. But the organization it calls forth is so powerfully adapted to it, that it thereby acquires a crushing, rare, direct, and monotonous splendor. Thus in all cases, at the bottom of the scale as at the top, on the lowest step of the temple as in its pediment, in the material as in the moral order, the beautiful and the useful mysteriously agree.

The official religious architecture is flooded with ornaments, quadrigas, bas-reliefs, allegories, and false columns. The Corinthian column which, with the leaves of its capital crushed by the entablature, was so illogical that the Greeks hardly ever used it, seems invented to permit the Romans to display, in stupefying contrast, the lack of artistic intelligence of those among them who were intrusted with preserving the city of art. As soon as they use ornament, their architecture loses its beauty, because it loses its logic. And the same error occurs every time they aim at effect before considering function. Here are silver cups of the Romans, their bowls cluttered with chiseled forms. One can scarcely drink from them. A lover of enjoyment and the positive life, the Roman goes astray when he approaches speculation, the general idea, the symbol. As soon as it is a question of satisfying his material instincts, he says admirable things.

There are no ornaments on his aqueducts, his bridges, or his thermæ, very few on his amphitheaters, and these are, with those positive portraits, his only real works of art. Bare, straight, categorical, accepting their role, they present to us their terrible walls, piles of matter gilded by the southern fire, crackled and whitened by the frosts of the north. They present their aërial vaults on cyclopean pillars, the lines of giant arches bestriding the valleys and the swamps, bursting through rocky barriers or sealing them—as sure, in their vertical rise or their progression, as cliffs or as herds of primitive monsters. The goal toward which they aim gives them a look of implacability. They have the inflexibility of mathematics, the force of the will, the authority of pride.

They have the lightness of the foliage that quivers at the top of the trees, sixty feet above the ground. The arch, the vaults of various kinds, the corridors, and the cupolas, a thousand blocks of granite are, for

ROME. Antonine column (II Century A.D.). Execution of the Germanic chiefs, detail.

twenty centuries, suspended in the air like leaves. They cannot crumble before the infiltration of water and the assault of the winds and the sun have uprooted their trunks; they have an air of being natural growths which would outlast all winters. To petrify the depth of the azure, the depth of the tree top! It needed the imagination of man to realize the miracle of offering to the crowds, as their perpetual shelter, the curves which bent over the curve of the earth. It needed the audacity of man to suspend matter in space by its own weight, to stick stones to one another by leaving so little space between them that they cannot fall, to check their tendency to separate by thickening the pillars that bear them, until a point of absolute solidity is reached.

The higher it is, the straighter it is; the barer, the denser; the less of light, the fewer openings and empty spaces it offers, the better the wall presents, on the smiling or dramatic face of the soil, the image of will, of energy, of continuity in effort. The Roman wall is one of the great things of history. And, as it is Might, it is Right. It seems to be uninterrupted, it holds forever, even when split and fissured. The fall of a thousand stones does not shake it. For ten centuries all the houses of Rome were built of the stones of the Colosseum. The Colosseum has not changed its form. The Roman wall remains identical with itself everywhere. The pavement of the roads, which for two hundred leagues pursues its rigid march, is only a wall lying on the earth to embrace it and enslave it. The arch of the bridges, which is only a wall bent like the wood of a bow, draws taut the passive bowstring of the rivers. The wall of the aqueducts, hollowed out like the beds of the rivers themselves, carried their waters in a straight line wherever the ædile wants them to go. High and bare, the outer wall of the theater prevents those whose appetite or rebellion is to be overcome from peering into the free expanse of the horizon. The wall of the circuses, continuous and compact as a circle of bronze, incloses the bloody orgy within the geometrical rigor of a law.

The Great Vestal (III Century A.D.).
(National Museum, Rome.)

The wall that rounds itself over the tepidarium and the swimming pools, with the docility of an atmosphere kept within in its spherical boundaries by the gravitation of the heavens, confers on voluptuousness and hygiene the grand authority of a natural order.

It was in Rome that the Pelasgic poem of the wall, developed so sensitively and wisely by the Greeks

Vase from the Treasury of Bernay, silver (*Bibliotheque Nationale*).

and the Etruscans, found its most powerful and durable expressions. It was in Rome that the applications of the Asiatic vault were the most various, its use the most frequent, its employment the most methodical. The vault, in Chaldea and in Assyria, had lengthened itself out, weighed down on the palaces and houses or swelled above them, and hung over the cities. In Rome it is the very base of every utilitarian construction, and the greater part of the architectonic forms derive from its presence—the arches of the bridges, the portals, the corridors around the circuses, the immensity of the halls made possible by the might of the walls, the power of the supports, required by the height of the edifice, the circular monuments—

GALLO-ROMAN ART (beginning of the III Century). Wild Boar (*Museum of Orleans*).

images of the horizon, of the plains bearing the cupola of the sky.

The Tombs of Cecilia Metella, the Mole of Hadrian, and the Pantheon of Agrippa especially, are epitomes of the force of Rome and of the severe and savage ring of hills, the circus in the center of which it is built. It is a sad power that it possesses; the full walls are as rough as the hide of a monster, the interior is as secret and jealous as the soul of this people, which did not consent to manifest itself before having stripped from every other people the right to discuss that soul. The thing weighs on the crust of the earth and seems to emanate from it. At the top of the Pantheon a circular opening lets in the light of heaven. It falls as if regretfully, and never succeeds in illuminating the farther corners. Rome is self-willed and closed.

It is only into the stone circuses that the sun entered in a flood, to light up the spectacles which the tamed world gave to Rome while it waited till it should gather up in the city its hatred, revolt, and thirst for purification. *Panem et Circenses!* The Colosseum is nothing but the formula in stone of the monstrous needs of the king-people. The patrician no longer has war at his command to occupy the plebeian. Here is bread—here are circuses, in which a whole city can be seated and which are built in such a way that from each of the seats one can witness the death struggle of that city. Never has there been seen under the heavens a theater better arranged for presenting the spectacle of a suicide than that one.

The equilibrium of Rome had not the spontaneous and philosophic character of the equilibrium of Athens, and this does not result so much from the multiform extent of the Roman Empire as from the depth of its moral anarchy. Greece, while at war with Persia, was much nearer to harmony than Rome was at the very hour when she decreed peace. Her repose, her art, her pleasure, even, were of an administrative order. The struggle of interests, the rivalry of classes, and the social disorder continued from the early days of

GALLO-ROMAN ART. Altar (*Church of Verecourt*).

the Republic to the triumph of Christianity. Throughout Roman history the poor man struggles against the rich man, who holds him, first by war, then by games. But below the poor man there was a more miserable being who rarely saw the games, save as an actor in them. This was the slave, the dark rumbling of Suburra and the Catacombs, and woman, another slave, outraged every day and by all, in her flesh and in her tenderness. The being who lives in the shadows ceaselessly calls upon the sun to rise within him. The mystic tide of the poor, the tide born of Hellenic scepticism was mounting and was to submerge Roman materialism. Rome did not dream, doubtless, that the day on which she broke the frightful resistance of the little Jewish people marked the beginning of the victory of the little Jewish people over herself. It was in the law of things that the soul of the ancient world, compressed by Rome, should flow back into the soul of Rome. The patricians had been dominated by the Greek ideal; the plebeians, in their turn, were dominated by the Jewish ideal.

The church was to be built on this hard stone, and the rich man was again to enslave the poor man by giving him the promise, or the simulacrum, of the well-being to which he laid claim. Rome, by becoming Christian, did not cease to be herself; as she had remained Rome when she thought she had become Hellenistic. The apostles had already veiled the face of Christ. Rome had no trouble in casting the feeling of the masses in the mold of her will to launch them anew upon the conquest of the earth. Her material desire for world-empire was to reawaken upon coming into contact with the dream of universal moral communion, which Christianity, after far-away Buddhism, implanted in the souls of men; and it was to transform this dream to its profit. Julian the Apostate, the last hero who appeared on the dark earth before the fall of the sun, thought he was combating the religion of

Cinerary urn (*National Museum, Rome*).

Asia. It was already against Rome that he was struggling, and Rome had the habit of conquering. The men of the north, flood after flood, may descend toward the Mediterranean, the great mirror of the divine figures, the inexhaustible basin of rays to which all the ancient peoples came to draw up light. Rome, buried under incessant human waves for more than a thousand years, is to remain Rome, and when she reappears at the head of the peoples, the peoples are to perceive that they are marked with her imprint.

GALLO-ROMAN ART (I Century A.D.).
Altar of Jupiter (*Cluny Museum*).

ALPHABETICAL INDEX

OF THE NAMES CITED IN THIS VOLUME[1]

Abraham, 117.
Æschylus, 119, 148, 176, 226, 247.
Agamemnon, 117.
Alexander, 110, 208.
Anaxagoras, 150.
Antenor, 152.
Apelles, 250.
Aristocles, 134.
Aristophanes, 156, 233.
Assurbanipal, 90.
Augustus, 218.

Baudelaire, xviii.
Bernini, xl.
Bryaxis, 201.
Brygos, 252.

Cambyses, 76.
Carrière (Eugène), xxvii.
Cervantes, xxix.
Cézanne, xli, xlii.
Clarke, xl.
Clexthas, 134.
Cyrus, 101.

Darius, 106.
Diderot, 254.
Douris, 252.

Endoios, 138.
Euphronius, 252.
Euripides, 194.
Evans, 116.

Giorgione, 251.
Guyau, xxiii.

Hagelaidas, 134.
Hannibal, 270.
Heraclitus, 160.
Homer, 116.

Ictinos, 176.

Jesus Christ, xxxiv, 226, 228.
Julian the Apostate, 303.
Juvenal, 270.

Kanakhos, 134.
Kant, xxiii.
Kock (Paul de), xl.

Lamarck, xxxiv.
Leochares, xl, xlii.
Lucian of Samosate, 212.
Lucretius, 270, 281.
Lysippus, 200, 223.

Maret, xl.
Masaccio, 248.
Michael Angelo, xviii, xxx, xl, xliv, 215.
Michelet, xviii, 292.
Moses, 117.
Mummius, 270.
Myron, 154, 156, 279.

Napoleon, xl.
Newton, xxxiv.

Parrhasios, 250, 251.
Pasiteles, 218.
Pericles, 156.

---

[1] The names of the artists who are directly in question are printed in Italics.

ALPHABETICAL INDEX

Phidias, xix, xxxiv, xl, xlii, xliv, 149, 150, 156, 162, 168, 176, 178, 194, 196, 210, 218, 226, 242, 246, 279.
Pindar, 148, 247.
Pisistratus, 128, 138.
Plato, xxiv, 150.
Plautus, 270.
Polycleitus, 154, 156, 279.
Polygnotus, 250.
Praxiteles, 192, 194, 196, 214, 224, 231, 279.
Pyrrhus, 270.
Pythagoras, 226.

Rembrandt, xviii, xxxiv, xlii, xliv.
Renoir, xli, xlii.
Rodin (Auguste), xxiv.
Rubens, xlii.

Saint Paul, 226.
Sargon, 90.
Schliemann, 116, 117.

Scopas, 201, 210.
Semiramis, 86.
Sennacherib, 90.
Socrates, 150, 226.
Solomon, 105.
Sophocles, 148, 176.
Spencer (Herbert), xxiii, xxviii.
Sully (James), 14.

Taine, xviii.
Theocritus, 246.
Titian, 251.
Tolstoi, xx.

Vergil, 270.

Winckelmann, xliii.

Xerxes, 140.

Zeuxis, 250.

SYNOPTIC TABLES

Roman altar (*Museum of Arles*).

SIGNS AND ABBREVIATIONS

Employed in the synoptic tables

a. Architect.	Sp. Spain.	A. Attic School.
s. Sculptor.	Af. Africa.	Ag. Argive School.
p. Painter.	A. M. Asia Minor.	Æ. Æginetan School.
c. Ceramist.	M. G. Magna Græcia.	S. Sicyonic School.

The names of painters, sculptors, architects, ceramists, and other workers in the plastic arts are in italics. The names of the principal masters are in heavy type.

Only such monuments are mentioned in the synoptic tables as still exist or of which there are fragments of sufficient importance to constitute a work which possesses interest from the artistic or archæological point of view. Exception is made in the case of destroyed monuments of particular celebrity, as the temple of Hera at Olympia (the earliest Greek temple known), the Colossus of Rhodes, the Tower of Babel, the Temple of Solomon, the Sanctuary of Eleusis, and the Asclepieion of Epidaurus.

GALLO-ROMAN ART (III Century A.D.). (*Museum of Sens.*)

B.C.[1]	Prehistoric Lands	Asia	Egypt
300th century (?)	Basin of the Garonne, Vézère-Pyrenees, etc. (Cave-dwelling reindeer hunters) Split-off flints		
200th century (?)			
100th century (?)	Arms and tools of bone Carved bones and stones (Bruniquel, Laugerie-Basse, Laugerie-Haute, Mas d'Azil, Lorthet, La Madeleine, Brassempouy, Baoussé-Roussé, Cro-Magnon, Le Moustier, Arudy, Gourdan, Lourdes, Cap-Blanc, Willendorff, etc.) Painted and engraved walls		
75th century (?)	(Combarelles, Fond de Gaume, Le Tuc d'Audoubert, Bernifal, La Mouthe, Marsoulas, Niaux, Salitré, Laussel, Comarque, Teyjat, Pair-Non-Pair, Covalanas, Castillo, Tortosilla, Homos de la Peña, Altamira, etc.)		
60th century (?)	Split-off flints		
50th century (?)			Carved flints Carved flints
40th century	Scandinavia, France, Switzerland (Lake cities) Polished flints	Chaldea[1]	Potteries Wrought metals Stone and ivory statuettes
35th century			

Greece	Rome	Geological Epochs[1]
		Glacial period
		Epoch of Aurignac
		Paleolithic epoch
		(Chelles)
		(Le Moustier)
		(Solutré)
		Magdalenian epoch
		Totemism
		Warm and moist period
		Neolithic epoch
		Totemism
		Sothic period, Classic calendar (4240)
		Hieroglyphic writing (?)
		Babylon. Astronomy
		Fou-Hi, Chinese legislator (3468?)

[1] The dates are merely approximations and may vary by many centuries.

B.C.[1]	PREHISTORIC LANDS	ASIA	EGYPT
33d century	Necklaces, Bracelets, Potteries	Observatory Temples (The Tower of Babel)	Ancient Empire [1] (*Memphis, I to X Dynasties*)
30th century	SCANDINAVIA,[1] FRANCE, BRITTANY, SPAIN, ENGLAND (*Megalithic monuments*) Menhirs	Engraved cylinders Palace of Tello Statues of Goudea Stele of the Vultures *Cheo-Hang* invents painting in China (?)	Sphinx of Gizeh, Thinite Hypogees of Abydos, Hieraconpolis and Negadyie Pyramid of steps at Sakkarah Temple of pink granite Archaic statues of diorite Pyramid of Meidoum
28th century			Hypogees of Sakkarah Pyramids of Gizeh
	Dolmens	Megalithic monuments in India	Mastaba of Gizeh Limestone statues Archaic paintings Mastaba of *Ti*, a. in chief, at Sakkarah Pyramids of Abousir
25th century	Triliths	The Chinese scale (?)	Mastaba of Ptahhotep at Sakkarah Apogee of sculpture and painting Pyramid of Ounos at Sakkarah Mastaba of Meri Pyramids of Sakkarah Seated Scribe of the Louvre
22d century		Temple of Ourou in Chaldea	MIDDLE EMPIRE [1] (*Thebes, XI to XVI Dynasties*)
21st century	Cromlechs	Code of the Laws of Hammurabi in Chaldea (on stone)	Obelisk of Heliopolis Hypogees of Sint Hypogees of Abydos Pyramids of Fayoum
20th century	Alignments	First Chinese bronze (?)	Great Temple of Amon at Karnak
19th century			Hypogees of Beni-Hassan Hypogees of Assaouan Apogee of jeweler's art and goldsmith's art Industrial and intimate art Pyramid of Dahchour
18th century	Covered alleys	First Chinese ceramics (?)	Classic funerary sculpture
17th century			The labyrinth (Temple of Haouara)
16th century	Megalithic monuments	Statue of Napir-Asou in Chaldea	Colossus of Sowakhotep III Sphinx of Tanis The bearer of offerings of the Louvre Hypogees, paintings
			NEW EMPIRE [1] (*Thebes, XVII to XX Dynasties*)
15th century	Megalithic monuments		Academic funerary sculpture Temple of Deir el-bahri
	Megalithic monuments		Temple of Amada First hypogees of Biban el-Moluk

GREECE	ROME	GEOLOGICAL EPOCHS [1]
		Menes founds the Egyptian empire (3300?)
		The great dike
ÆGEAN PERIOD [1] (*Crete, Argolis, Archipelago, Troy*)		
Cyclopean walls Palace of Phæstos in Crete		Exploitation of the mines of Sinai
Pelasgic walls		*Cheops, Khephren*, Pharaohs
Wrought metals, potteries (*Troad*)		The House of the Books
		Dynasty of the *Hia* in China (2205)
		Abraham. The patriarchs of Israel
Terra cottas (*Troad*)		The Hebrews in Egypt (?)
		Power of Sidon. Cuneiform writing (?)
Vase of the reapers of Phæstos		Lake Mœris (?)
		Conquest of Nubia by the Egyptians Invention of papyrus (?)
		Invasion of the Hyksos in Egypt
Palace of Tyrinth (Bas-reliefs, frescoes, pottery)		The Aryans in India (?)—The Rig-Veda (?) Egypt expels the Hyksos
Marble idols		The Mesopotamian canals (?)
Palace of Knossos, Crete (Bas-reliefs, frescoes, pottery)		*Minos*
		Vasya (?)—The Mahabarata (?)
		The Phœnicians invent the alphabet

[1] The dates are merely approximations and may vary by many centuries.

B.C.[1]	PREHISTORIC LANDS	ASIA	EGYPT
14th century	Megalithic monuments		Speos of Gebel Silsile Hypogees of Cheik el Abd el-Kourna *Senmout*, a. Colossuses of Memnon Temple of Amenophis III at El-Kab Temple of Luxor Hypogees of El-Amarna Temple of Sethos I at Kourna Temple of Sethos I at Abydos
13th century	Megalithic monuments	Phœnician textiles, potteries, and glass Hittite art	Great hypostyle hall of Karnak **Meïy**, a. in chief of Thebes The Serapeum The Ramesseum Colossus of Rameses II Great temple and colossuses of Ibsamboul Cavern-temple of Gerf-Housem Temple of Beit-el-Oualli Temple of Hathor at Ibsamboul Temple of Seboua Speos of Derr Restorations of monuments Hypogees of Biban-el-Moluk Temple of Khonsou at Karnak Great temple of Rameses III at Medinet Abou Tomb of the Queens at Medinet Abou Hypogees of Biban-el-Moluk
12th century	Megalithic monuments Bronze weapons and tools	First Chinese jades (?)	
11th century	Bronze weapons and tools Bronze weapons and tools	Cypriote art *Hiram*, Phœnician, a.	Jewelry—Goldsmith's art Industrial and intimate art
10th century	Bronze weapons and tools	Temple of Jerusalem	Saite Empire (*Delta, XXI to XXX Dynasties*) (950)

Greece	Rome	History
		Conquest of Assyria by the Egyptians
Mycenean potteries		*Moses.*—The Hebrews depart from Egypt
		Power of Tyre
		Rameses II (Sesostris ?) (1330?-1265?)
Treasuries with cupolas Palace of Mycenean		
Gate of the Lions at Mycenean Potteries, terra cottas		*Rameses III* (Sesostris?) (1230?-1200?)
Treasury of Orchomene		Trojan War
Tombs of Mycenean (Jewels and masks of gold)		
Vases of Vaphio		Chou Dynasty in China (1122) The judges in Israel
		Invasions of the Dorians in Greece and in Crete
HELLENIC PERIOD		
		Homer
		David (999-959)
		Solomon (959-929)
First terra cottas at Tanagra		Nineveh

[1] The dates are merely approximations.

B.C.[1]	Prehistoric Lands	Asia	Egypt
9th century	Bronze weapons and tools	Assyria Zigurats (towers of stages) Hanging gardens Bas-reliefs (Monsters, winged geniuses, kings and warriors, scenes of hunting, and war animals) Engraved cylinders Palace and bas-reliefs of Nimrod	Jewelry—Goldsmith's art Industrial and intimate art
8th century	Bronze weapons and tools	Palace and bas-reliefs of Khorsabad Palace of Zindjirbi Palace of Dour-Sharroukin	Industrial and intimate art **(Egyptian Renaissance)** Seated chiefs of cities
7th century	Megalithic monuments Bronze weapons and tools	Palace and bas-reliefs of Koujoundjick Reconstruction of the Tower of Babel	Portraits Restorations of temples Jewelry—Goldsmith's art Industrial and intimate art Statuettes of women

Greece	Rome	History
		Elijah—The prophets in Israel
Dipylon vases at Athens		*Lycurgus* in Sparta (884) *Assurnarzipal* (885-860)
		The Jehovist. Genesis (?)
		Struggle of the Assyrians and the Hittites
		Founding of Carthage
	Etruscan art	*Hesiod*
Xoana (wooden idols)		Era of the Olympiads (776)
		Archilochus
(The Doric Order)	Funerary urns	Founding of Rome (753) Era of Nabonassar (747)
Temple of Hera at Olympia		*Isaiah* (774-690) *Sargon* (722-705) Greek colonies in Italy and in Sicily
Corinthian vases		*Sennacherib* (705-681) destroys Babylon (692)
Rhœcus and *Theodorus* mold in bronze	Etruscan paintings and tombs	Conquest of Egypt by the Assyrians (671)
First coins		*Assurbanipal* (667-25)
Feminine statue of Eleutherna (Crete)	**(The Tuscan Order)**	*Tyrtœus*
Temple of Selinus (628), M.G.		
Artemis of Delos		
Mikkiades, s. of Chios	Etruscan vases (Importations from Greece)	
(The Ionic Order)		Laws of *Draco* (614)
Chersiphron, a. of the first temple of Ephesus A. M.		The Phœnicians make the tour of Africa (609) The Medes destroy Nineveh (608)
Temple of Corinth		*Jeremiah* (650-590)
		Founding of Marseilles (600)

[1] The dates are approximate.

B.C.	PREHISTORIC LANDS	ASIA	EGYPT
			Statuettes and portraits
		MEDO-PERSIAN EMPIRE (*Assyro-Egypto-Ionic Art*)	
		Reconstruction of the Temple of Solomon	
6th century	Megalithic monuments Bronze weapons and tools		Jewelry—Goldsmith's art Industrial and intimate art
		Palace of Persepolis	
		Tomb of Cyrus at Pasargades Bas-reliefs of Behistoun	
		Apadana of Susa Bicephalous bulls Frieze of the archers and the lions	
	Megalithic monuments		
		Tomb of Darius at Persepolis	
		Monuments of Istakhr	
5th century (First half)			Jewelry—Goldsmith's art Industrial and intimate art

Greece	Rome	History
(Argos, Sicyon, Sparta) Vases (black on red) *Polymedes*, Ag. s. Dorian Apollos		Founding of Cyrene (598) Nebuchadnezzar (604-561) rebuilds Babylon (597) Solon (594)
Dispoinos and *Skillys*, Cretan ss. Hera of Samos (580) Temple of Zeus at Syracuse, M.G.	The Cloaca Maxima of Rome (Etruscan)	The Pythian games (586) Captivity of Babylon (585-535). The Isthmic games [*Ezekiel* *Alceus*, *Sappho*
Archemos, s. of Chios Temple of Selinus, M.G.		*Empedocles*
Nike of Delos *Cleothas* and *Aristocles*, S. ss. *Kanakhos*, S. s. Polygonal wall of Delphi *Ergotinos*, *Klitias*, *Exekias*, c. and p.		*Zoroaster* (?) the Avesta (?)
Basilica of Pæstum, M.G. Statue of Chares Parthenon of Pisistratus *Hagelaidas* Ag. s.	Etruscan paintings and tombs	*Lao-Tsze* (604-529)
Endoios, A. s. The Moscophorus *Boupalos* and *Athenis*, ss. of Chios Temple of Apollo at Delphi	The she-wolf of the Capitol (Etruscan)	*Sakyamuni* (The Buddha) (?) *Pisistratus* (560-527) *Anacreon* *Cyrus* (560-29) takes Babylon (538)
Vases (red on black) The treasury of the Cnidians at Delphi	Black stone of the Forum (?)	*Heraclitus* (576-480) *Cambyses* (529-22) conquers Egypt (528)
Eumaros, p. Orantes of the Acropolis *Bathycles*, s. of Magnesia Great temple of Herakles at Agrigentum, M.G.		*Pythagoras* (552-472)
Stele of Aristion Temple of Metaponte, M.G. **Antenor**, A. s. The Tyrannicides	Temple of Tarquinius Superbus at Rome (509)	Athenian Republic—Roman Republic (509)
(Athens) Calon A.E. s. Temple of Ægina		*Confucius* (*Kung Fu Tze*) (551-479) *Theognis* of Megara *Aristides* (540-468)
Glaucos and *Dionysos*, Ag. ss. Ephebe of the Acropolis *Cimon* of Cleonæ, p.		*Darius* (521-485) Athens repulses Asia Marathon (490). *Miltiades* (?-489)
Hegias and *Micon*, A. s. Temple of Demeter at Pæstum, M.G. *Panœnos*, Ag. p. Demeter of Eleusis *Glaucias*, A.E. s.	Etruscan tombs	Sack of Athens. Salamis (480). *Themistocles* (525-459), Platæa, Mycale (479). *Pausanias* (?-474) *Æschylus* (525-456) *Pindar* (522-442)

B.C.	PREHISTORIC LANDS	ASIA	EGYPT
	Bronze weapons and tools		
		Tombs of the Achemenides	
			Herodotus visits Egypt
	Megalithic monuments		
5th century (2d half)		Hispano-Phœnician bust of Elche	
	Bronze weapons and tools		
	Megalithic monuments		

Greece	Rome	History
Pythagoras and *Onatas*, A.E. ss.		Rebuilding of Athens
Terra cottas of Tanagra		
Dancers of Herculaneum		*Cimon* (?-449)
Temple of Hera at Agrigentum, M.G. The Charioteer of Delphi (462) *Libon*, a. of the Temple of Zeus at Olympia (460) (Centaurs and Lapiths) The long walls (460-445) *Critias, Nesiotes,* and *Calamis*, A. ss. Temple of Zeus at Agrigentum, M.G. **Polycleitus**, A. s. Temple of Concord at Agrigentum, M. G. Theater of Syracuse, M.G. **Myron**, A. s. The Discus Thrower Temple of Neptune at Pæstum, M.G.	Etruscan walls of Norma and of Matri (?)	*Pericles* (494-429) Hegemony of Athens
The Theseion		The Law of the Twelve Tables at Rome
Phidias, A s. (490-431) **Ictinos**, A. a. of The Parthenon (447-32) and the sanctuary of Eleusis *Alcamene* and *Pœonios*, A. ss. *Polygnotus*, A. p. *Agoracritus*, A. s. *Douris, Euphronios,* and *Brygos*, A. cc.		
Temple of Segesta, M.G.		*Sophocles* (495-406)
Mnesicles, A. a. of The Propylæa (437)		*Herodotus* (484-406)
Temple of Cape Sunion		
Theater of Segesta (?), M.G.		*Euripides* (480-406)
Temple of Zeus at Nemea		*Democritus* (490-380)
Sicilian coins, M.G.	Etruscan tombs	*Thucydides* (471-401)
Jewelry—Goldsmith's art Industrial and intimate art		*Socrates* (469-399)
Temple of Phigalia (419)		*Alcibiades* (450-404)
The Erechteion (415)		Wars of the Peloponnesus (431-404)
Kallimachos, a.		
(The Corinthian Order)		*Aristophanes* (455-388)
Temple of the Wingless Victory		
The Dancers of Delphi		*Hippocrates* (460-380)
Euryelus of Syracuse, M.G. (402-397)		Hegemony of Sparta
Bas-relief of Leda (Athens)		
Stadium of Delphi (?)		Retreat of the Ten Thousand (399). *Xenophon* (445-354)
Polycleitus the Younger, a. of the Theater of Epidaurus *Daedalos*, A. s. *Asclepicion* of Epidaurus		Rome taken by the Gauls (390-389) *Epaminondas* (415-362)

B.C.	PREHISTORIC LANDS	ASIA	EGYPT
4th century	Bronze weapons and tools	Palace of Firouz-Abad in Persia Hispano-Phœnician art The Hindoo scale Palace of Sarvistan in Persia Phœnician sarcophagi of Sidon	Jewelry—Goldsmith's art Industrial and intimate art Portico of Nektanebo at Philæ
3d century	Megalithic monuments	Stupa of Sanchi in India Columns of Asoka in India *Lie-Y*, Chinese p. The great wall of China (246)	PTOLEMAIC EMPIRE Temple of Debot Jewelry—Goldsmith's art Industrial and intimate art

Greece	Rome	History
Agatharchus, p. and decorator discovers perspective **Zeuxis**, A. p. *Apollodorus*, A. p. **Parrhasios**, A. p. *Eupompos*, p. *Cephisodotus*, A. s. **Scopas** *Bryaxis* and *Timotheos*, A. ss. of the Mausoleum of Halicarnassus, A.M. (352) Apogee of the Tanagras *Pamphilos*, Macedonian, p. *Pythios*, Ionian a. Theater of Dionysos (?) The Niobides Monument of Lysicratus (335) Temple of Priene, A.M. (334) Second temple of Ephesus, A.M. *Leochares* and *Euphranor*, A. ss. Demeter of Cnidus Temple of Lycosoura **Apelles** (356-308), A. p. *Silanion*, s. Apollo of the Belvedere *Nicias*, A. p. **Praxiteles** (360-280), A. s. *Aristoxenes of Tarentum* (350-?) *Philon*, a. of the Portico of Eleusis (311) **Lysippus**, A. s. *Hermogenes*, a. of the temples of Magnesia and of Teos *Pausias, Protogenes* and *Aetion*, p. p Didymeion of Miletus, A.M. Venus, Psyche of Capua, M.G. HELLENISTIC PERIOD (Asia Minor) (Islands, Alexandria, Cyrenaica) The Sarcophagus of Alexander, A.M. Victory of Samothrace *Chares*, s. Temple of Apollo at Delos Colossus of Rhodes *Timomachos*, p. *Polyeuctos*, s. *Epigonos*, s. of Pergamum Terra cottas of Myrina, A.M. (*Diphilos*, coroplast) The Dying Gladiator	Etruscan tombs Etruscan tombs *Fabius Pictor*, p. Appian Way (312) Sarcophagus of Scipio Barbatus (298) First silver coins (269) Rostral column of Duilius (260) Etruscan tombs	*Plato* (429-348) Hegemony of Thebes *Demosthenes* (385-322) *Aristotle* (384-322) *Philip* (359-336). Hegemony of Macedonia (338) *Mencius* (*Meng-Tze*) (?-314) *Alexander* (356-323) conquers Egypt and Asia Minor and penetrates into India *Valmiki* (?) The Ramayana The Ptolemaic Empire (323) *Zeno*. Stoicism Founding of Alexandria (305) *Manetho*, Egyptian historian The Museum of Alexandria *Euclid* Rome subjects Etruria Epicurus (331-270) *Pyrrhus* against Rome (280-274) Rome becomes mistress of Italy (270) First Punic War (264-41) *Asoka*, King of India (277-23), becomes a Buddhist *Archimedes* (287-212)

B.C.	Prehistoric Lands	Asia	Egypt
	Bronze weapons and tools	Sarcophagi, potteries, masks, and jewels of Carthage (Africa)	Temple of Isis at Philæ Temple of Edfu (237-212—176-122)
2d century	(?) Prehistoric sculpture (stone) (Gaul, Spain) Megalithic monuments Bronze weapons and tools Coins and bronzes of Gaul	(India) Temple of Kandajiri Greco-Buddhistic sculpture Temple of Bhaja Chaitya of Karli (163) Temple of Ajunta Stupa of Bharhut Bas-reliefs of Hiao-Tang-Chan in China Temple of Buddha-Gaya in India (?)	The trilingual stone of Rosetta (196) Temple of Kom Ombo Temple of Hathor at Philæ Alexandrian Temple of Esne Sanctuary of Osiris at Karnak
1st century	Weapons, coins, and bronzes of Gaul	Hebrew sarcophagi	Alexandrian Temple of Hathor at Dendera Roman kiosk of Philæ (18) Roman temple of Homs at Kalabche Restorations of temples

Greece	Rome	History
The Sleeping Fury Jewelry—Goldsmith's art Intimate sculpture	Cist of Ficoroni (*Novios Plautius*, bronzeworker) Flaminian Way (220)	*Ptolemy III* fixes the length of the year as 365¼ days (238) *Theocritus*
Cleomenes, s.		*Hannibal* (**247-183**), Second Punic War (218-02) Rome subjects Magna Græcia and Sicily (211)
Alexandrian	art	*Plautus* (250-184) *Antiochus the Great* (222-186). Power of Antioch
Seated pugilist of the Thermæ		*Philopœmen* (233-183)
Damophon, s. (Statues of Lycosoura) art		*Ennius* (240-169) *Hipparcus*, astronomer
Isigonos and *Stratonicos*, ss. of Pergamum Altar of Pergamum, A.M.	*Pacuvius* (220-130), p.	*Judas Maccabeus* (200-160) Invention of paper in China (?)
Theater of Delphi	Aqua Marcia (146)	Destruction of Carthage (147) Greece becomes a Roman province (146)
Timarchides, *Polykles*, The Venus of Milo (*Hagesandros* ?, s.)	Greek ss. at Rome	
Ctesibios invents the organ		*Tiberius* and *Caius Gracchus* (133-121)
Euboulides, s.		
Andronicos Cyrrhestes, a. of the Tower of the Winds, Athens	*Mutius*, a.	*Marius* defeats the Cimbri and the Teutons (102-101)
(**School of Rhodes**)	Importations of Greek works at Rome	*Sylla* (126-**78**)
Apollonios of Tralles, s. of the Farnese Bull	Roman copies of Greek works Aqueduct of Tarragona	*Lucretius* (98-55) Revolt of the slaves at Rome—*Spartacus* (73)
Agesandros, s. of the Laocoon	*Coponius*, s. *Titidius Labeo* and Arellius, pp.	*Lucullus* (109-57) against *Mithridates* *Cicero* (106-43) [(135-63)
Apollonios, A. s. of the Hercules of the Belvedere art	*Vitruvius*, a. and critic The Aldobrandini wedding	*Cæsar* (100-44) conquers Gaul (51)
(**Roman School**)	Tomb of Cecilia Metella	
Pasiteles, s.	The Edility of *Agrippa* (33) The Palatine-House of Livia	*Vergil* (70-19)
The throne of Venus (?) *Stephanos*, s.	The Pantheon of Agrippa (26) (*Valerius of Ostia*, a.) Pont du Gard (19)	*Augustus* (63+14)—The Roman Empire (31)
Venus of the Esquiline (?)	Ludius, p. Theater of Marcellus (13) Pyramid of Cestius (12)	*Horace* (65-08)
Glycon, s. of the Farnese Hercules	Tomb of Vergilius Euryaces Kabr er Roumya, Numidian tomb in Algeria	*Titus Livius* (—59+19)
Dioscurides, mosaist, M.G.	Sarcophagi Busts and statues	
	Bridge of Rimini (14)	
Amphitheater of Pozzuoli (?), M.G.		*Jesus Christ* (—04+29)
Menelaos and *Archelaos*, ss. (Roman School)	Arch of Triumph of Orange	*Philo the Jew* (—30+54)
	Amubius, p.	*Strabo*

A.D.	Prehistoric Lands	Asia	Egypt
1st century			Alexandrian
2d century		Bas-reliefs of Ou-Leang-Tze in China Tsai-Yong, Chinese p.	Necropolis of Alexandria Gate of Hadrian at Philæ Alexandrian Sarcophagus portraits

Greece	Rome	History
	Theater of Taormina, M.G.	
Crouching Venuses	Theater of Saguntum (?), Sp.	Greece pillaged by the Romans
Venus of Arles	Mausoleum of Saint-Remy (?)	
	Quintus Pedius, p.	*Seneca* (2-65)
	Art of the Catacombs	
art	Alexandrian art	
	Aqua Claudia	*Saint Paul* at Athens (54)
	Turpilius, p.	
	Pliny the Elder (23-79), critic	*Nero* (54-68). Burning of Rome (64)
	Maison Carrée of Nîmes	The Emperor *Ming-Ti* becomes a Buddhist (64)
	The Coliseum	
	Monuments of Herculaneum and Pompeii, M.G.	
	Arch of Titus	
Sculptures, paintings, and industrial art of Herculaneum and of Pompeii, M.G.		Taking of Jerusalem by the Romans (71)
	Arena of Pola	
		Destruction of Herculaneum and Pompeii (79)
Aristeas, *Papias*, Greek ss. at Rome	*Frontinus* (40-103), engineer	*Josephus* (37-?)
	Arena of Arles	
	Monuments of Cherchell, Af.	
	Amphitheater of Saintes (?)	*Juvenal* (42-?)
		Tacitus (55-117)
	Lacer, a. of the Bridge of Alcantara (105)	*Epictetus*
Apollodorus of Damascus, Greek a. of Trajan		*Trajan* (98-117)
	Golden Gate of Pola	
	Trajan's column (112)	
	Gate of Benevento	
	Bridge and monuments of Mérida	
	Aqueduct of Segovia	
Monument of Philopappos	Bridge of Salamanca	*Plutarch*
	Monuments of Timgad, Af	
Arch of Hadrian at Athens		*Hadrian* (117-138)
	Temple of Baalbeck, A.M.	
Cossutius, Roman a. of the Olympieion (134-35)		
	Nonius Datus, a. of the Aqueduct of Cherchell, Af. (137)	*Lucian of Samosata*
		Ptolemy, astronomer
	Amphitheater of Treves	
	Aqueduct and waterworks of Zaghouan, Af.	
art	Alexandrian art	
	Mole of Hadrian	
	Theater of Orange	
	Art of the Catacombs	
	Arena of Nîmes	
Pausanias visits Greece	Capitol of Dougga, Af.	Roman Embassy in China (166)

A.D.	Prehistoric Lands	Asia	Egypt
3d century		Chaitya of Amravati in India Stupa of Sambrunath in India (Nepal) Tsao-fou-hing, Chinese p. Bridges of Dizfoul and of Chouster in Persia Bas-reliefs of Sapor at Nakch-e-Roustem	
4th century		Fortress of Gwalior in India Iron column of Delhi Buddhistic frescoes of Turkestan First porcelain tower at Nankin (China) Kou-K'ai-Tche, Chinese p.	Sarcophagus portraits

Greece	Rome	History
	Arena of El Djem, Af.	*Marcus Aurelius* (161-180)
	Column of Marcus Aurelius (180)	
Odeon of Herod Atticus		
	Monuments of Djerach, Af.	
	Septizonium of Septimius Severus	*Kalidasa* (?). The Sakuntala (?)
	Arch of Septimius Severus (203)	
	Arch of Triumph of Lambessa, Af.	
	Arch and Temple of Tebessa, Af. (214)	*Tertullian* (160-240)
	Theater of Aspendos (?) A.M.	
	Art of the Catacombs	
	Statues of the Vestals	
Alexandrian art		*Plotinus* (205-70)
	Busts, statues, sarcophagi	
	Colonnades of Palmyra, A.M.	
	Walls of Aurelian at Rome (271)	*Aurelian* (270-75)
	Temple of the Sun at Palmyra, A.M. (273)	
	Arena of Verona (296)	
	Palace of the Thermæ at Lutece	
	Column of Pompey at Alexandria (302)	
	Thermæ of Diocletian at Spalato	*Constantine* (306-37). Triumph of Christianity
	Arch of Constantine (315)	
	Basilica of Constantine	*Byzantium* (326)
	Arch of Janus Quadrifons (?)	
	Gate of Treves (?)	*Julian the Apostate* (361-63)
	Church of Saint Paul outside the walls (386)	*Saint Jerome* (331-420) *Theodosius the Great* (378-95) destroys the pagan idols (383) *St. John Chrysostom* (347-407)
		The Visigoths destroy Eleusis (395) End of the Olympic games (396) *Hypatia* (370-415)